Silver and Golden Campine Chickens
Chicken Breeds Book 26

by F.L. Platt

with an introduction by Jackson Chambers

Introduction

I am pleased to present yet another title in the "Chicken Breeds" series.

This volume is entitled "Campines" and was authored by F.L. Platt in 1914.

The work is in the Public Domain and is re-printed here in accordance with Federal Laws.

Though this work is a century old, "Campines" contains much information on poultry that is still pertinent today.

As with all reprinted books of this age that are intended to perfectly reproduce the original edition, considerable pains and effort had to be undertaken to correct fading and sometimes outright damage to existing proofs of this title. At times, this task is quite monumental, requiring an almost total "rebuilding" of some pages from digital proofs of multiple copies. Despite this, imperfections still sometimes exist in the final proof and may detract from the visual appearance of the text.

I hope you enjoy reading this book as much as I enjoyed making it available to readers again.

Jackson Chambers

A. F. Lydon 1898
The Feathered World

DUCKWING.

PILE

BLACK-BREASTED RED.

BIRCHEN.

BROWN-BREASTED RED.

GAME BANTAMS.

(Specially drawn to illustrate Mr. Proud's articles on Bantams.)

Vincent Brooks, Day & Son, Ltd., Lith

BLACK ROSECOMB.

JAPANESE.

SILVER AND GOLDEN SEBRIGHTS.

BANTAMS.

BRAHMAS.

WHITE ROSECOMB.

BOOTED.

INTRODUCTION

IT IS THE PURPOSE of this book to put before the reader in quickly accessible form the knowledge that expert breeders and judges have gained from their wide experience.

The contributors to this book were pioneer Campinists, and the work that they have done in refining and beautifying the breed is very great. But—it is very recent.

Much slower, and with great thoroughness, Nature had fashioned in her hand—according to the climate, soil and environment—the Campine race. Nature alone can make thorough-breds, and the Campine, with ancient lineage and pure pedigree, is one of Nature's thorough-breds.

Today the Campine is in the noontide of its popularity and perfection. Beginning with its early history, we may see it emerge from the shadows; we may see the rising sun of civilization disperse the vapor and mist of the dawn and the Silver and Golden Campines take distinct form on the sandy plains of the old Netherlands.

The wish of the editor is that this book will be worthy of the breed's high traditions, and that readers will find their expectations fulfilled.

One feature of the book that particularly impresses us as valuable, comprises the pictures of the leading winning specimens at America's foremost poultry shows. By observing these fine half-tone illustrations throughout the book, you will be able to study the progress that has been made from year to year in type and color, and note the trend of the times.

F. L. PLATT.

INDEX

The Campine

The Origin of the Campine—Its Economical Qualities—Early Crosses That Were Made—The English Consider 3½ Pounds for Hens and 5½ Pounds for Cocks the Normal Weight—A Roomy House is Required for Campines, and the Breeder Must Be Careful Not to Overfeed

By Rev. E. Lewis Jones, Heyope Rectory, Knighton, Radnorshire, England

UNDER this name—the Campine—we designate a breed that has its origin in Belgium, and is derived from two varieties there—the Campine and the Braekel. These two are very similar in marking, but differ in size (the Braekel being the larger), in type, and in certain other characteristics. The Braekel and the Campine must have come originally from the same stock (undoubtedly the Campine is a stunted Braekel), and have varied under the influence of environment, and through infusion of the blood of the races already in the districts when they were introduced into their present habitats.

The history of the breeds is unknown. They may have been in Belgium when Julius Caesar visited the place, and maybe they were the birds the old soldier took back with him to Rome, and which the Roman epicures much enjoyed. Undoubtedly, the Campine and Braekel are the G. turcica of Aldrovandus. We know for certain that these two were the noted breeds of Belgium of 400 years ago. The parent stock hens have a long, egg-laying pedigree, and I may as well say here that the English Campine has gained rather than lost in egg-laying power since its introduction into England. It has gained because we have bred for the character of egg-laying just as we have bred for improvement in markings of feathers. I say this because at present certain people in England and abroad delight in libeling the English Campine. It passes my comprehension why they should thus bear false witness against the bird as they persistently do. Not only have we improved the prolificacy of the bird, but we have more than maintained the size of the egg. There is no means of getting at the traducers of the English Campine, except thus to expose them.

The bird, as introduced into England, differed a good deal from our present exhibition bird. The male had practically a white top, and the tail was black. The females were not at all well barred, and in a few cases were the colors separate. To breed good cockerels and good pullets according to the Belgian standard means double-mating, and the English Campine Club decided that it was not desirable that Campines should require double mating; so they determined to standardize the male similar to the female. I think they were wise in this decision, because they avoided double-mating, and because to standardize the male similar to the female means to strengthen the economic quality of the female—in this case, egg-laying. I need not here tell again how the greatest Belgian poultry authority, the late Monsieur L. Vander Snickt, was converted to the truth of this by re-

membering how similar the males were to the females amongst the cattle of Denmark, where cows are noted for their milk-producing qualities.

The English standard Campine is, then, a bird with white neck hackle, the rest of the body barred, the black bar being as near as possible three times as wide as the white ground color, and certainly not less than three times as wide. The white ground color must be open and bold, not narrow threads, something like fine cobwebs, going across a black body. Each feather should end in a clear white bar. The barrings should suggest rings round the body, the geometrical exactitude being broken by the rounded ends of the feathers. The dividing line between the colors in the bar should be clearly defined and straight, not dovetailing or zig-zagging in any way. Most certainly the bar should not be curved, or in the shape of a horseshoe. The direction of the bar may vary—that is, it may run transversely or obliquely across the feathers. What is important is that the edge colors should be clean cut and distinct. The oblique direction of the bar is very pretty, giving rise to what is described as mackerel markings. All that I have so far attempted to describe I call the regularity of the markings. This regularity gives exceeding beauty to the bird, and here very often judges go wrong, placing a bird forward because he is heavily marked, disregarding much

BRAEKELS

An ideal pair (1900) from drawings forwarded by the secretary of the Braekel Club of Belgium to "The Feathered World," England.

more regularly but less heavily marked birds, which are in reality far ahead.

Now we must examine the individual feathers, and the first point is the distinct white tip. Then we look to see if the colors are pure—the white white, without any intermixture of black or grey; the black black without a tendency to an intermediate bar of very narrow gray in the middle of the black. This is most important, and yet I have seen it largely disregarded by specialist judges. The gray bar is a fatal fault, and I would never breed from such a bird, even if he looked a picture of beauty. I have seen birds win under specialist judges with this fault, birds that I would not use in the breeding pen even if they were sent me as a gift. I have been surprised myself sometimes to find what I considered almost a waster, that I had sent in only to make the number up, finishing well in the money, and my best bird somewhere amongst the "condemned" or cardless. The black should be covered with beetle-green sheen, which gives the bird a magnificent iridescent appearance in the sunshine, and the contrast between the silvery white and the sheen really makes the beauty of the breed. Sometimes the sheen is purple, and such birds

should not find their way into the money, and should be discarded as breeders. I have spoken of the body markings first, because I consider them most important. I divide the plumage into three parts—(1) hackle, (2) breast, and (3) saddle and tail, and I have placed them in order of difficulty of attainment, though I really think (1) and (2) are about equally easy. Any man who wants to breed good Campines must look first to the color and regularity on top, wing bar, saddle and tail. In breeding, if you hit that, you will find it easy to combine with it a good white hackle or a good breast, but I have not yet had the three together with each nearly perfect. Now, why do I say the top, wing bar and saddle are the most difficult? See illustration, page 5, and you will see these were originally white, and the potentiality in the bird is towards whiteness there. A bird with good hackle and good breast, but weak on the parts mentioned, is at best a poor one, not hard to breed, but useless as a breeder. Such birds have sometimes won. It is not my intention to explain the mating of Campines, but only to give certain suggestions for the breeder to work out himself scientifically.

I have said enough about the plumage, and will turn to other points. In type I insist on a good carriage in the cock, and a well-rounded breast in both sexes. Looking down upon the bird, I like a wedge-shaped individual, broader across the shoulders than across the saddle. I like a fairly long back, and the saddle well finished with feathers. The tail should be well developed, fan-shaped in the females, and in the male furnished with two long sickles. It should incline 40 deg. to the horizontal. The head points now require attending to. We have hitherto spoken of the body markings, and have not touched on these points. I like the comb to be well set on the head, and where it leaves it to proceed slightly under the horizontal, as if it meant to follow the nape of the neck, but thought better of it. There should be five or six serrations, and these should be pencil and not wedge shaped. The comb should be medium, of fine texture, and free from creases of all kinds. I like

Rev. E. Lewis Jones; his home in the Welsh hills; a bird's-eye view of the rectory and poultry farm; a shipment of Campines at the railway station, cooped for exportation to his American agent, J. Fred N. Kennedy, and some of the beautiful birds that Rev. Jones has bred.

to see the back part of the comb of the hen falling over, and not so heavy as to affect the sight. The wattles should be medium, of neat shape, and fine texture. The earlobe should be white, and I think more than one-third red should disqualify.

Campines started in England as exhibition birds about 1899, and it was not until 1904 that anything like a standard cockerel was shown. This bird was bred from eggs sent over by Monsieur Oscar Thomaes, of Renaix, Belgium. Dr. Gardner placed him first, etc., at club shows at the Alexandra Palace, 1904. Now the showing of this bird aroused a great controversy. How was it bred? The answers were all equally various and equally wrong. The fact is there is a tendency amongst the birds in Belgium towards markings on the back, but the Belgians only preserve the white topped ones breeding only from such birds, and destroying the others. I wish to pay a tribute to the magnificent appearance of the white-top bird, but the necessity of studying the best interests of the breed tempers my regret at his being displaced by the favorite standard male.

Economic Qualities

If the Campine is to obtain the popularity which everything seems to point to now, it is as a utility bird that it is to do so. Its three characteristics are: (1) Prolificacy; (2) size of egg; (3) hardiness. It combines these three qualities to a greater extent than any other breed. Again, it lays steadily all the year round. Since I have kept Campines I have never been without an egg. As a table bird it is delicious; it carries a great deal of breast meat, and ratio of offal to the weight of the bird is as small as in any breed. The bone is fine, thus resembling the wild Game birds. As a milk chicken nothing beats a Campine cockerel nine weeks old or thereabouts. It is a good table bird where quality and not quantity is the desideratum. It is, however, as a layer that the Campine must come to her own or fail, and since I have been hon. secretary of the Campine Club every change in the standard has been in the direction of intensifying the laying powers of the bird.

Mating, Feeding and Housing

Campines breed very true. The first point is to select the male; and I have already mentioned ideal markings, so need not repeat what I have said. Select the females to suit the male, remembering that the male is largely responsible for regularity and purity of markings. Type is the first consideration in selecting females.

The great thing is not to overfeed. They are active birds. They do well in confinement; mine have been for the last six years in runs 10 yd. by 20 yd., and I think I can claim they have not suffered. But the bird is a great forager, and thrives exceedingly well on a free run, when it will pick up three parts of its feed. There is no special system of feeding required, and I find that the only thing necessary is ordinarily wholesome food.

The birds require a roomy house at night if they are to thrive. They should get at least 10 cubic feet each. Feeding and housing have a lot to do with their prolificacy, and I have often known people run them down when the real fault was in their own mismanagement and overfeeding.

The eggs hatch well and the chickens are strong and healthy. They grow well and feather quickly, but they are exceedingly active, and if there is any mischief for them to get into they will get into it, and the result is mortality. In rearing chickens the one thing to guard against is long, wet grass, for they will surely find their way into it and get soaked to the skin, and such a wetting is fatal to any young animal. I advise three feeds of dry food to one of wet for the youngsters.

WINNER OF FIRST, MADISON SQUARE GARDEN, NEW YORK, DEC. 31, 1912 - JAN. 1-4, 1913 WINNER OF FIRST, BOSTON.   JAN. 7-11 1913 BRED AND OWNED BY MANHATTAN FARMS, BRIGHTON, N.Y. U.S.A.

Interest in Campines has reached a high point at Madison Square Garden. The most progressive breeders from both sides of the Atlantic have there lined up the best birds obtainable. At the 1913 exhibition the cockerel pictured above stood out as the beauty of the class. In color he was well ahead of all the rest, as everyone admitted at New York and when he reached Boston, the critics had to admit that he had outgrown the slenderness that might have been criticised at the earlier show. Such birds will do much to increase the already phenomenal popularity of the breed.—F. L. Sewell.

The Normal Size for Campines

We hear a great deal about the size of the Campine, and in shows they do vary, for some are derived from the smaller Belgian Campine, and some from the larger Braekel. The smaller birds, both in Belgium and England, are better marked than the larger ones, and so the judge has to balance up between size and markings. Personally, I think if a bird is big enough to pass the minimum it should get full marks for size, and that markings should then decide. I have written in Feathered World, London, on "Mere Size," and I have seen nothing to shake the views I there expressed that there is no real gain in excessive size.

As a rule weight comes from bone, and bone is expensive to build and useless as food. The English Club decided that 3½ lb. for hens and 5½ lb. for cocks was the normal weight; this was a pious expression, not a standard pronouncement. I think this is high-water mark myself, and I should strongly oppose any further addition. Those who have bred Campines are in the best position to know the right weights. I do not want to confuse size and weight or to create such confusion in the minds of my readers. We must remember there is an economic weight for every breed; exceed this, and nature revenges herself by decreased prolificacy or decreased size of eggs or both. We do not want to rouse Madame Nature.

Hamburg Crosses

I do not suppose just now an article on Campines would be complete without some mention of this. We are told freely that our birds show evidences of crossing with Hamburgs. Now, I should confess that, as a humble student of Mendelism, I have no repugnance towards crossing, and I should not hesitate to cross if I saw any advantage in so doing. I will further confess that I have tried every way of crossing that I could conceive of, and with the result that I got nothing that it would pay me to introduce into my strain. When persons say that my exhibition strain shows evidence of Hamburg crossing, they are talking arrant nonsense—a nonsense which shows they do not understand the possibilities of Campine breeding or of what a Hamburg-Campine cross looks like. We must bear in mind that in the Hamburg we have highly developed and complex marking, the result of at least half a century of breeding. When you cross with a Campine you let loose all the centrifugal forces kept in check by breeding in a definite direction, and the results are amazing. Were breeding such a simple thing that equal black and white on the Hamburg could be immediately transferred into three blacks to one white on the Campine or something near, or even if we could keep the Hamburg regularity, then breeding would be so easy that many of us would

A CAMPINE-PHEASANT HYBRID

This spirited looking bird I saw on the poultry plant of Rev. E. Lewis Jones, in Wales. It is a hybrid that came from the crossing of a pheasant and a Campine. It has proved unfertile with members of either parent species and should Rev. Jones produce others they probably would follow the usual rule and prove unfertile among themselves. The word "hybrid" is derived from a Greek word which translated means "an insult or outrage, and a hybrid has been supposed to be an outrage on nature, an unnatural product." As a general rule, birds belonging to different species do not produce offspring when crossed with each other, and when they do breed, the progeny are termed hybrids, while the word mongrel is used to name the common product of crossing distant varieties of the same species. Rev. Jones has made a number of crosses among the varieties of domesticated poultry. He is a close student of Mendelism and he is a personal friend of Bateson. The first chapter in the new edition of Lewis Wright's Poultry Book is a chapter on Mendelism by the Rev. Jones.

prefer to play marbles. From 1899 to 1903 Campines were in the hands of some of the most skillful breeders of the day, and had the Hamburg cross been a short cut to the Campine standard a clear back bird would have been exhibited before 1904. Most people who write this Hamburg cross nonsense are mere babies in arms in the matter of breeding to the veterans who bred Campines twelve years ago. However, the problem is simply stated. Cross Hamburg and Campine, and you have four things to outbreed: (1) Red eye; (2) size of eggs; (3) type; (4) penciling. It requires a man skillful above the average to make that cross successfully, and I should feel proud had I been able to achieve it. Again, a Hamburg has a red eye, but no one will contend that every red-eyed Campine is the product of this cross. Further, in the years Hamburg fanciers have been breeding, they have not had a good wing bar. Campinists have, and it is one of the Campine's special points of beauty. Did this come from the Hamburg cross?

I have not the space to discuss all possible crosses, but the conclusion of the whole matter, from my short experience is, that you cannot cross the Campine with any hopes of success. I do not say it cannot be done, but only that I do not know the way to do it, and I shall be glad to hear of a way, providing I can examine the birds. I have heard many tales, and I always put to the test any theory, however fantastic it may appear to be, for one never knows; it may be a pearl of price, even if out of a toad's mouth, as the Welsh proverb has it. My experience has made me very sceptical indeed of the wonderful results to be had from crossing. If the Campine is the bird I think it is, then there is no means of crossing it without deterioration.

If the reader has not tried Campines—well, let him give them a fair trial, and keep them for, say, three years, until he has come to understand the breed, and I feel sure that he will be as devoted to them as I am.

The Braekel and Its Eggs

The Braekel Has the Reputation of Being the Best Egg-breed in Belgium—The Braekel Eggs Bring an Income
of $1,600,000 a Year to That Small Part of Belgium Where the Braekel Hen is Kept—Russia
Wants to Know How to Increase the Size of Her Eggs—The Quality of the Braekel's
Egg—How the Eggs are Packed, a Thousand in a Basket—A Report by
A. F. Hunter of a Trip Through the Braekel Country is
Commented on by the Author

By Louis Vander Snickt, Brussels, Belgium
(Being compiled from Monograph of "The Braekel Fowl", by M. Vander Snickt, and translated by Madam A. F. Van Schelle)

THE Braekel hen has for centuries enjoyed the reputation of being the best among egg-laying breeds, and the market of Nederbraekel, a township situated in the midst of the district of Alost, enjoys the reputation of producing eggs of the best quality, in fact dealers of eggs recognize that these eggs weigh 3 grams more than those of any other market, and are superior in flavor—hence it follows that these eggs always bring a higher price than any other eggs.

As a tree is judged by its fruit, so an egg-laying hen must be judged by her eggs. Therefore, instead of beginning as fanciers have done until now, by speaking of full grown chickens and old breeding cocks, we shall turn our attention to their products, by beginning with the Braekel egg, its importance for agriculture and trade. Then passing by the industry of rearing milk fed chickens, to grain fed chickens, to the selling of egg-laying chickens we shall arrive naturally to the choice of breeding stock and the judging of these different varieties of a pure breed, of which the gray with white neck-hackles is the type most generally appreciated and most widely diffused, especially in the Alost district and its immediate neighborhood.

This type, probably original and called silver, subdivides itself into two varieties with white necks; one having the plumage of the body barred and that of the other flowered. A third variety is black headed, called Sottegem. These three varieties exist in the gold: namely gold instead of silver and there is still a seventh called chamois, also with golden ground, but in which the black markings have given way to white. There are also entirely white Braekels, black and consequently a blue variety. All of these varieties have existed and still can be obtained with short legs and are subdivided according to size. The large Braekels, called Grammont, for sex positions; the medium sized ones for eggs in farms and the small ones bred outside the rich soil of the Alost district, called Campines, because they are bred on the poor sandy soil of Campine.

The Braekel is the hen adapted for centuries to the district of Alost. The inhabitants select it for the quality and quantity of its eggs. It has its characteristic forms

THE LATE LOUIS VANDER SNICKT

and colors which they wish to keep, the colors, and the details of the markings of the plumage are secondary.

Quantity and Value of Braekel Eggs

It is no easy task to obtain by statistics exact figures on the commercial movement of eggs in the interior of the country. We paid a visit to Mr. Desire de Mulder, ex-dealer in eggs and butter, and the most competent authority, in order to get exact and practical data about these two articles in the part of the country where he lives. We told him "Sottegem being the market which you know the best, as during all your life you have visited all the markets, how many eggs were sold there and at what price?" (That is a question which it is difficult to answer; the number of thousands of eggs brought to the market varies according to the seasons and the weather. The same condition applies to prices.)

"I want the average prices."

"If I answer your question by a figure you shall be the first to be astonished by the answer." We had just come back from Nederbraekel where the Braekel Club had just awakened from a long sleep and there we had been told that the trade of eggs from Braekel hens had taken such an extension in that township that not only are they sold by car loads, but twice a week, Wednesdays and Saturdays whole trains of eggs are sent out. In fact, I deem that in 25 years in the district of Alost the production of eggs has tripled.

"How many eggs come to the market of Sottegem every Tuesday in January?"

"That depends upon the weather."

"Then give us the average, if you please."

Now in December and January 50,000 at 15 to 16 centimes per egg. Five times fifty thousand is two hundred and fifty thousand and at 15 centimes that makes the sum of 57,500 francs. ($11,500.00.)

January—5 times 50,000 equals 250,000, at 16 centimes, equals 50,000 francs.

February—4 times 100,000 equals 400,000, at 10½ centimes, equals 42,000 francs.

March—4 times 175,000 equals 700,000, at 7 centimes, equals 49,000 francs.

April—4 times 200,000 equals 800,000, at 6½ centimes, equals 52,000 francs.

May—4 times 150,000 equals 600,000, at 6½ centimes, equals 39,000 francs.

June—4 times 150,000 equals 600,000, at 7 centimes, equals 42,000 francs.

July—5 times 150,000 equals 750,000, at 7½ centimes, equals 56,250 francs.

August—4 times 100,000 equals 400,000, at 8 centimes, equals 32,000 francs.

September—4 times 100,000 equals 400,000, at 9 centimes, equals 36,000 francs.

October—5 times 75,000 equals 375,000, at 10½ centimes, equals 39,350 francs.

November—4 times 50,000 equals 200,000, at 13½ centimes, equals 27,000 francs.

December—5 times 50,000 equals 250,000, at 16 centimes, equals 40,000 francs.

Total 52 weeks equal 5,725,000 eggs, price 492,025 francs. ($98,405.00.) The markets of Nederbraekel, Audenarde, Renaix, Grammont, Ninove, Alost, Gand, have the same importance as Sottegem. The Nederbraekel eggs weigh almost three grams more than the others and are sold at a higher price; moreover the Braekel eggs of Alost and Audenarde are the cleanest, for the reason that ground being more solid, sticks less to the claws of the bird.

Quantities of smaller markets for eggs have been established, such as Seenhuyen, Osterzele, Lierd de St. Marie, Esschen, St. Lieven, and others. It can be calculated that to one great market there are four small ones, and that in the four small markets they sell as much as in one large one. Thus there must be sixteen markets as important as Sottegem in the Braekel country. On this small territory there are annually brought to market 91,600,000 eggs, say nearly 8,000,000 francs go directly to the pocket of the small producer. ($1,600,000.)

The egg market of Wavre is twice as important (if numbers alone are considered) as any of those just spoken of. The eggs taken to this Braboncon market are sold for less money, because they weigh 7 grams less than those of Nederbraekel. However, if the Belgian fanciers had taken the trouble to busy themselves with the excellent Brabancon hen, as has been done for the last fifty years for the Braekel, the production of eggs in the Walloon Brabant would have been the envy of Oriental Flanders. This increase of 5 grams per egg would have been paid for extra in the market of Wavre alone.

When in 1900, the Belgians were invited to assist at the Avicultural Congress in St. Petersburg, his Imperial Highness, Great Duke Nicolawitch, said: "Gentlemen Aviculturists of different countries producing eggs, we have invited you to come to give us your advice; if thanks to your science we can increase by two grams, each egg laid in Russia, the resultant effect will be to augment by several millions of roubles, the income of the empire." We were proud to have been able to say, "Try our Braekel hen, and if this one cannot become acclimated after having left its orchards and the damp meadows of Flanders, try the Brabancon."

Braekel eggs which are quoted as first quality weigh 60 kilos the thousand, those of the Nederbrackel market weigh 3 kilos more, and those of the market of Wavre in Brabant, the largest market in Belgium, 7 kilos less. This difference of three grams between the Nederbrackel and the Sottegem produce in favor of the market of Nederbraekel makes a difference in the receipts of 28,625 frs. for the same number of eggs. This does not mean that Braekel eggs weigh an average of 60 grams. Pullet's eggs which are also carried to market are not so big as the eggs of hens two and three years old. One day Mr. de Mulder selected among 10,000 eggs 100 eggs of 80 grams with one yolk (these were not double yolked eggs.) These eggs were hatched at Mr. Gustave Boel's at the castle of Chenois at Mont St. Guibert. Happily being invited to select and to form a lot destined to populate the old farm at the mill of Ryperot at La Roche, we choose all the silver Braekels.

About that time, we had not yet succeeded in getting free from the influence of exposition fanciers, who had derived their inspiration from England instead of studying and following what takes place in Belgium and had been taking place a long time before the institution in England of exhibition fancy poultry. The judges of these shows will tell you without hesitation that the prize-winners must have on their plumage certain shades, and a certain number of regulation marks, but they carefully guard the source from which these regulations have sprung, and what is their influence on the production of eggs. The truth is that these gentlemen of the "fancy" care as little about an egg as a fish does about an apple. They rear chickens after a settled standard agreed upon with no other object than gaining prizes in expositions and selling at high figures the prize winners or those that merit a prize award. After having, during a few years, obtained as much money as possible with a few birds as near the standard as possible, and before having given the time to breeders to produce quantities of birds capable of gaining prizes, the standard is revised; the old type is out of style. We invite our friends, members of the Braekel Club to keep away from that sort of trade of a doubtful nature. That is why, instead of beginning by inducing them to give an undue importance to the marking of the plumage, we begin by calling attention to the value of the egg of the Braekel hen whatever may be the color of her plumage. The majority of Silver Braekels selected to start breeding in Ryperot were rose comb, exactly like those that characterize a breed created in view of taking part in expositions, known in England under the name of Red Cap. (Rood kap, Chaperon rouge).

This race exhibited in England is not a sub variety of the Braekel, it seems rather to be a variety of the Bergilsche kraher (Bergsche krooter, chanteur du berg, also of Elberfeld). Amongst the Braekel cocks, red-caps, of the Ryperot, there were some whose comb was separated like a needle had taken a development which had become as unseemly as the colossal simple comb of the Minorcas, which was the rage two or three years ago. After having committed the fault of putting aside all the Braekels, black, yellow and others, as well as the crosses produced from eggs weighing 80 grams, we still persevered in giving our preference to single combs. But in spite of this severe sifting, most of the progeny of the next generation reverted to rose combs. This proves conclusively that in certain farms in the neighborhood of Sottegem there exists a variety of Braekel with red caps which are inferior to no others for the production of the finest eggs.

The reputation acquired by the Braekel hen in St. Petersburg at the first Congress of Aviculture and at the great International Exposition, has not passed unnoticed in England. Great Britain was represented in

Russia by Mr. Edward Brown, professor of aviculture in the University of Reading and residing at the experimental farm of aviculture in Theale, belonging to the university; secretary of the National Society for the amelioration of utility poultry, and also of the section of the Smithfield Club, which organizes every year the show of dressed poultry, under the patronage of Sir Walter Gilby, Baronet.

The Braekel had already been seen at the Smithfield, England, Club Show, not for its eggs, but under the form of milk chickens, exposed by the principal merchants of Brussels, and grain fed chickens, after having been put for ten days to fatten, selected and dressed in the fashion of the country by Mr. Ceutrickx of Alost. The last year we were successful in obtaining permission for the Braekel breed to be represented by a cock and a hen alive, as well as a couple of Coucou de Malines by the side of specimens of the English races most renowned for their flesh.

Mr. Brown in company with Mr. Hunter of America (A. F. Hunter, associate editor R. P. J.), paid us a visit one day in Brussels in order to be shown how aviculture is carried on in Belgium. We spent three days in the district of the Malines, and the three of us made each a separate report, each of us having seen from a different point of view. Our three reports went around the world. Mr. Brown having returned to England, we went with Mr. Hunter to the egg district, the district of Alost, where the Braekel is on its native ground. We went on a Tuesday to the market of Sottegem. Mr. de Mulder, was kind enough to show us the workings of an egg market, as it is carried on today and as it was carried on in the time of Charles V. (Charles V. was king of France from 1364 to 1380). We saw how the eggs were brought, how they were delivered and paid for, how they were packed, a thousand in a strong basket and forwarded without any danger of being broken. This we have found admirable. But an Englishman and an American sees this from an entirely different point of view, with an eye distraught because with him the dominant idea is "with us all this is better done." Notwithstanding these gentlemen have remembered the theories exposed during our excursions the influence of blue pigment on the flavor of eggs and flesh, of the yellow pigment on resistance against disease and the effects of humidity, of the development of the comb on the production of eggs, the crowing of the cock on precocity.

The Congress of St. Petersburg took place in May. In the following year in July there was held a congress of aviculture in Reading, England, Ireland and Canada were represented. We were the only continental representative. We limited ourselves to explaining the theories about Belgian races, but especially that of the

Braekel. After one or two years the Braekel had acquired its title of nobility in England, it was put in the class of exhibition (show) breeds, but in spite of the laudable efforts of Captain Roger and of myself they have been accepted under the false name of Campine, and instead of being judged by the scale of points dictated by the Braekel, it is scaled by fancy characteristics.

At the Congress of Reading, where we went to uphold the old theories of breeding always respected in our district of Alost, we enjoyed the reputation of being versed on the subject of egg-laying chickens. Colonel Allsopp took us aside to put the following questions:

LOUIS VANDER SNICKT IN THE SHOW ROOM

We are delighted with the very excellent likeness of the late Louis Vander Snickt, by Artist F. J. S. Chatterton, which shows this faithful old friend of poultry culture in a characteristic attitude, judging the Black Whiskered Bantams at the Utrecht, Holland, Show. With tireless interest in highbred fowls, M. Vander Snickt spent his life in promoting their progress and the success of those who care for them. Studious consideration is expressed in the face and the hands hold the diminutive specimen with kindly enjoyment while examining its fine qualities and comparative value in the class. M. Vander Snickt has been one of the principal judges at Utrecht and other leading shows on the continent for many years, besides proving himself amply capable in poultry matters of advising with the king or directing the farmer or the peasant to more profitable methods of rearing poultry for the market. His sensible ideas of Standard-bred fancy fowls have given distinction to the true old races of Belgium. When directing the Zoological Garden of Ghent, or when in charge of the new Zoo of the Dusseldorf, or as editor of Chasse et Peche of Brussels, his fondness for fine fowls always impelled him to give them a prominent place in his life's valuable work.—F. L. Sewell.

"What advice can you give me to help me find the best egg-laying hen?" My answer was prompt, "Colonel," I said, "go to the market and buy the finest eggs for hatching and the chicks which will be hatched from those eggs will lay eggs similar to those of their mother." The colonel took a step backwards and made a profound bow. We asked why that ceremony, and he said, "Monsieur, when any one makes so sensible an answer it is well worth a mark of respect."

During the Congress of Reading, the rector of the university invited the members and the leading people of the city to his home. During the evening I had the chance to see exhibited in the same place all the kinds of eggs such as are found every day on the market of London, packed in a special manner and labelled to show the weight and price of each parcel. The eggs from France were the biggest, the finest and the best cared for, and brought the highest price. We vainly searched for the Braekel egg, packed by thousands in their wicker baskets. We heard after our return that the eggs of the Alost district do not go to England, because they bring on our market as high a price as the dealers can sell them at in England. There come very eulogistic reports from Denmark on the system applied in that country by co-operative societies which collect and deliver their eggs in England. Thanks to the jealous care which the Danes take to guarantee their honesty and the freshness of their eggs and butter, they have succeeded in obtaining in England for Danish eggs the highest price paid proportionately to the quality of the merchandise.

But so far nothing has been found to compare with our admirable markets. Since the foundation of the Braekel Club at Nederbraekel, three similar societies have been formed in the Alost district, one at Erembodeghem, Dender Kieken at Orammont, and de Zwarte-kep at Sottegem. Following the advice given by the National Federation we have studied in harmony with the society of Erembodeghem whose members bind themselves to devote their efforts exclusively for the sale—as much as possible in common for the sale—of their products, eggs, chicks, pullets and hens. Before taking steps to favor the foundation of an egg syndicate, we have taken the advice of Mr. de Mulder. The latter answered us that the eggs laid by the hens belonging to the members of the syndicate would never be in sufficient numbers to make competition against established markets, that, besides, intelligent farmers would prefer to sell direct to the market and dealers rather than to accept the control of such an organization.

Quality of the Braekel Egg

After all, the dealer in eggs is the best judge of an egg-laying race; it is he who contributes the most to the amelioration of the race in a practical way. These dealers are in direct communication with the producers and they do not only complain, but they pay less when the eggs are too small, too long, too dirty, too fragile, or not answering in every detail to the exigencies of the consumer. These observations by being frequently repeated and all the more by being weighted by a money consideration are taken into account by the farmers, and when they see that a neighbor returns from the market with a cent more for each egg, they are not slow in selling the old hens and replacing them with hens of the variety of the neighbor, or even with the same family of hens.

The quality required for an egg of the Braekel hen can be enumerated as follows: The shell is white, not glossy and solid. The envelope which coats the shell is so strong that when the egg is cracked or even partly crushed in a basket the white does not run. The white of the egg is very thick, elastic and keeps the yolk well in place, so as to make the Braekel the best of all for poaching. The pellicle holding the yellow is sufficiently thick so that in breaking the egg the yellow remains intact. The yolk of the Braekel egg is generally thicker in proportion to the white than that of other eggs. It is more highly colored. When the hens of different breeds have been deprived of liberty and food, the yellow of the eggs laid under those conditions will become paler, whereas the yolk of the Braekel egg will longer retain its fine deep color and its good savor, and the hen will lay longer than any others. But the hen herself will grow weaker and waste away and conse-

quently is more subject to microbic diseases, whose germs are spread everywhere and await but the anemic condition of the organism which favors their development and they are overcome by disease. (Good care of the birds is necessary.) The size of the yolk of the egg corresponds to the external form of the egg. When two eggs of ordinary size are broken lengthwise, of say 60 grams each, one being of round form and the other oval, the yolk of the round one will be one-fourth larger than that of the other. The size and the quality of the yolk of an egg are of great importance in its value. The confectioners in order to make certain pastry take 18 Braekel eggs, but when they are obliged to take other eggs they need, in order to obtain the same result, to break another six eggs, of which they use only the yolk.

This explains why the eggs quoted by the thousand at Sottegem at (even dearer at Nederbraekel) 15 to 16 centimes apiece, are paid for there on the market, direct to the farmer, higher than we pay for eggs in retail at the shops in Brussels. In Brussels many of the eggs are received from the Wavre market, from isolated farms, from dealers of packed eggs or from small syndicates which will vainly endeavor to compete with the markets of the district of Alost.

The flavor depends on many things.

Packing

Eggs are packed in straw, the freshest and cleanest possible. Look at the packing of a thousand eggs in wicker baskets serving for a long period of time for their transportation. The dexterity of the good people employed for that work in taking only good eggs, in manipulating them without ever breaking one, in placing them firmly so that not one can break is simply admirable. They avoid carefully placing a basket of eggs beside fish. The food of the hen and the physical condition in which she is, exert their influence in a curious way. It suffices that a hen should eat something of a peculiar taste, say for instance onions and immediately her egg will taste of it; the eggs laid in damp weather differ from others. The eggs with the finest flavors come from hens running free in prairies and orchards on the loamy soil of their native districts. The race and the color of legs and other details still unknown have their influence on the flavor of the egg. When last year we had the opportunity of doing the honors at the Avicultural Exposition of Brussels to the ambassador of the Chinese empire, this gentleman stopped with pleasure before the "Negresse" chicken with white, silky plumage (Silkie.) He seemed to enjoy similar feelings to what one experiences when encountering a compatriot in a foreign land, and took pleasure in saying that this breed is highly appreciated in China for nothing else than for the delicacy of flavor of its eggs. This information from so reliable a source but confirms an old theory of the district of Alost. It is due to the blue legs of the Braekel cockerel, the grain fed-chicks have a fineness of flavor—the belief is widely current. This peculiar flavor is developed in cockerels at three months of age and capons. It is already noticeable in Braekel eggs. Our deep respect for the theories of the ancients has made me deem childish and ridiculous the pretensions of some foreign fanciers who have tried to impose upon us fancy standards bearing upon the markings of the feathers to the detriment of the production of eggs. These gentlemen take their inspiration from England, ignoring the Braekel hen, whose eggs have been the subject of the preceding paragraph.

Let us begin by putting aside certain details of plumage which would be childish if the importance paid to the feathers had not delayed for twenty years the practical development of a race which has been the fortune of its native district. Before busying ourselves with the pretended perfection of markings of some of the numerous varieties of plumage, characteristic of the Brackel (this phase will be treated exhaustively at the opportune moment) we insist that the leg should be blue, the beak blue, sometimes clear horn color at the extrimity, the eye should be black, the eyelid blackish. The Braekel should have an expression of face bohemian, almost like a "negresse," and this excess of black and bluish pigment on the face has unquestionably some connection with the quality of the egg. At all events, more relation than the ridiculous question of more or less bars on the back of the cocks, which in our time had no bars at all. Transported to another region than its nativity, on whose soil and in whose climate it was formed and to which it was adapted, the Braekel loses a great part of its value because not being in its natural environment, its activity is spent in entire loss. From the moment of hatching its instinct induces it to find its animal food where it cannot exist, and to ignore the kind of natural food found by the hen already adapted to its new environment, that is why the Braekel will languish where other indigenous breeds would prosper.

Even its reputation for laying is proof that the Braekel is "the queen of egg layers." The justification to this title has just been given chemically to the avicultural university of Gembleux. The chemical analysis of the different eggs and of eggs of chickens of different races has been made so as to ascertain the relation between the composition of the food absorbed and the egg produced. Eggs of hens that have had animal food are the richest in phosphate and in axotic elements. The diminution of richness in the elements of eggs is about in proportion to the diminution of animal food found by the hen. But the Braekel hen makes exception even after being deprived of strengthening food; vital elements are still found in its eggs. Then these axotic elements found in the egg, not being able to be produced from the food absorbed, can but come from the hen herself. The Braekel not finding sufficient food to form her egg, nourishes it to her own detriment from her body, and naturally at the expense of her proper health, and to her power of resistance against disease.

It is always interesting and instructive to know the opinion of foreigners. In 1897 we made an avicultural excursion with Mr. Edward Brown, of England, and Mr. A. F. Hunter of America. This gentleman has published in Farm Poultry in Boston, (of which Mr. Hunter was then editor) the following account: "We took the train from Sottegem on a market day in order to see the peasants bring their eggs and the dealers buy them. There were hundreds of salesmen, some a foot carrying the eggs in a basket hung over their arm, some driving a horse hitched to a cart, some again in a little cart drawn by three dogs, but all having eggs and butter. None had eggs in great quantities; three, five or eight dozen. But small rivulets make large rivers; it is thus that in this season they take every Tuesday to the market over two thousand eggs. Of course, they come in smaller quantities in winter. The town of Ghent receives ten times as much as the market of Sottegem, and there are thus in Belgium a great number of townships and villages whence leaves a great flow of eggs for England and the great towns, such as Brussels and Paris."

Let us state that the Britishers and sometimes Americans have their preconceived ideas; show them, explain to them, anything you like, they will remain firm in their own conviction that the mass of eggs which passes through Belgium for the English market is laid in Belgium. (The fact is that the Braekel eggs go largely to France, particularly to Paris; also to Brussels). Continuing, Mr. Hunter says:

"I have seen there a man who buys and sends to England 25,000 eggs every week. And I was introduced to a dealer, Mr. de Mulder, who buys every week 10,000 to 20,000 eggs for his own shop of eggs and butter in Brussels. We entered a large room of the town hall, where are delivered the eggs that he buys on the market; they are packed ready to be shipped by train to Brussels. The eggs are packed in large baskets of oblong shape and are very strong. A layer of straw is placed at the bottom. The sides are coated or lined with straw, a layer of eggs, a layer of straw, another layer of eggs, another layer of straw, and so on. A covering of sacking is attached to make every thing fast and is sewed to the borders of the basket. The size of the eggs was wonderful; they were uniformly large, of an immaculate whiteness, a collection of eggs in which nothing more could be desired. Perhaps one in a hundred was cream color, and this one was invariably smaller. I took one in my hand for curiosity, and I was told immediately how this one is never as good; it comes from a cross of Cochin. These eggs, slightly tainted, and a bit smaller are sold cheaper and are put aside. The fine brown eggs that we have in America are not known here. In examining the eggs on the markets of Brussels I have noticed that they were slightly soiled, evidently by the straw in which they had been packed; this must happen when the straw is slightly wet. It is sure that the eggs that you see on the markets of Brussels are less clean and attractive than those that I have seen in Sottegem."

Mr. de Mulder has informed us that the cleanliness of eggs depends on the nature of the soil. Dealers of eggs are intelligent enough to make use of only clean straw of first quality. Again, Mr. Hunter says:

"In passing before the hotel of the dealer who sends to London we went in to see his way of packing. His eggs are put in boxes containing each 1600. It is exactly the same method used for transportation in baskets. When the last layer of eggs is placed the top layer of straw is higher than the rim of the box. The lid is firmly pressed and nailed, so that no egg can budge. The eggs seem exposed to be crushed, but I was told that it seldom happens that a single egg is bruised. I could not help thinking that our system of boxes and cardboard compartment was far superior, facilitating the counting and packing. However, here the packers manipulate the eggs with an incredible rapidity." (There is an example of Anglo-American self sufficiency. Mr. Hunter is willing to acknowledge that he never saw eggs handled with such dexterity. In spite of that he still prefers cardboard boxes. He does not ask how it would be possible to send in two hours' time 2000 eggs packed in separate boxes. According to recent experiments the shell of the egg has an average thickness of 0mm 35, pressed at the two ends it can support a medium weight of 26 kilos. It can support an external pressure of 30 to 40 kilos, and an internal pressure of 2½ to 4¼. "An excursion in the neighborhood of Sottegem has proved to us that everywhere could be found the same flock of ten to twelve and two or three breeds of chicks around each habitation. It is from these innumerable small flocks that we receive these great quantities of eggs sold on the markets of Belgium.) "In the district of Malines few eggs are taken to the market, for nine out of every ten are very likely placed under the hen for the production of the fine table poultry, which is the specialty of that district. At .Sottegem, it is the contrary, almost all of the eggs are taken to the market and few are used for breeding."

(Here the kind of hens is just as much a specialty as the Coucou de Malines is in that town. Here it is the Braekel. This species is almost identical to the Campine, and has probably the same origin, but it is a bit larger, less of a vagabond, and lays eggs remarkably larger. The difference between the two breeds could easily have been brought about by the selection of large eggs and in discouraging the propensity of running far. As nobody keeps a report of the number of eggs obtained, it is impossible to know anything more than an estimation of the production. They have counted on nine francs ($1.75) profit per hen (this is the estimate of Mr. Louis Limbosch, who had Braekels at Esscheme, Dutch boundary). This would be about the total production of the hen, for the flock finds for itself its feed except when it is bad weather; hence eggs give but a small profit. The price of the best (the largest) was at 5.25 francs the hundred at the time of our visit; at the time of their great scarcity it climbs up to 15.00 francs." This was taking place in 1897—within six years the price increased one franc.) "It is to be remarked that this is about the price in New England and the Middle States. If we estimate at two cents as the medium price the year round this annual profit of nine francs would be for 90 eggs sold annually at the market. If we allow 30 eggs per hen for breeding and for consumption in families we shall arrive at 120 eggs per hen, which is all you can expect from hens that seek their own food.

"Compare this with the 186 eggs laid by about 200 hens kept according to the system of semi-liberty, and we think that the advantage is entirely in favor of the American system. I firmly believe we shall attain the 200 eggs a year for each hen, by selection and careful breeding, and then there will be no more question of the system of semi-liberty. However, this question must not be discussed now. We shall come back to it later.

"Everywhere I go here I hear the country people talk in favor of breeding along the lines of race amelioration. The peasants and the farmers are breeding by nature; they have the instinct of breeding transmitted since centuries. They review the ancient breeds, they perfect them by selection and by care. There is a lot to be done. Italian (Leghorn) blood got infused in nearly every flock. There results a yellow coloration of legs and skin and a diminution in the size of eggs. The tendency towards reversion is a great help for the reconstitution of the Campine and the Braekel and breeders expect from it great profit. In the country, the general habit is to go the "estaminets" and during the eve-

ning while taking a glass of beer peasants speak of the experiments and exchange their ideas. There are also guilds (or societies) and the result of all this is to transmit to youth knowledge acquired by the elders and the best established principles of breeding are transmitted by the passing generation to those who follow in their footsteps. One of their elementary principles is that the first pullet (the precocious ones) are not good egg layers. They arrive too early at maturity and then after laying a few eggs, want to brood and it is difficult to prevent them from doing so. The moral of all this is, that you must sell the precocious pullets as 'poulets de grain' (petits poussins or squab broilers, that is chicks as big as squabs as we call them in the United States) and keep the next brood for egg layers.

"The Campine and Braekel have been named everyday layers. A hen was brought to us that was said to be a specimen of a layer of fine big eggs; she resembled very nearly the Bolton Gray such as it was 40 years ago. The dark gray with some traces of spangled (half moon) cream, white neck hackles; the wing when open very dark with several flight feathers almost black; the eyes and eyelids black; beak and legs blue, ear-lobes bluish white, crest hanging and resembling greatly that of the Leghorns and Minorcas. She was remarkably long in body and almost as heavy as a game hen. We were told that when these hens ceased to lay they have naturally become fat, weighing six to seven pounds apiece, and are sold then at the market at three to three and a half francs each.

"A great encouragement to the amelioration of breeding stock here is the high price paid for eggs uniformly large. The breeder appreciates the strength of this argument. When he sees "Ricus" obtain for large eggs 16 sous a dozen, whereas "Boone" gets only 14, he begins to reason and makes the resolution to breed only such hens as lay eggs that can be sold at the highest prices. 'Utility' is their motto, they don't care for fancy poultry nor for the breeder who puts plumage, crest or earlobes and shape before the eggs. 'Utility' and the points for a fancier are always conflicting a Flemish man told me in a conversation that I had with him in Sottegem. Fancy breeders spoil the races from the egg-laying and practical standpoint, because they always breed by selection according to the selection of beauty of feather. We leave them the Bantams, the Cochins, the Brahmas, also if they like; they are not 'practical' races, but they should leave alone our Braekels and our Campines—and common sense would say that our Flemish friend is right."

During the time that has elapsed since this sensational article was inspired here and written and published in America, enormous progress has been realized. We shall not say in one, but in every respect. The Braekel in the beginning of the new century has succeeded in beating the record of the world. And chance enables me to prove that this record can be established and recorded in round figures.

The Rapid Progress of the Campine.

What Legend and History Have to Tell Us of the Origin of the Campine—Its Sister Breed, the Braekel—
In 1884 Separate Classes Were Made for the Two Breeds in Belgium—A New Type Introduced
Into England in 1904 and Improved English Birds Imported to America in 1907—
The Advancement Made in Color and Style—Its White Eggs Win at Boston—
Description of An Ideal Campine Section by Section

By F. L. Platt

THE Campine is a fowl that was bred in times that are now long past. In the ornithology of the Italian naturalist, Ulysses Aldrovandus, which was published in 1599, there is a description of the G. turcica or Turkish fowl, which indicates its strong resemblance to the modern Campine. Some four hundred years before, according to legend, the common ancestors of the Campine had been imported into western Europe by "Johana of Constantinople."

Antedating this, there is another tradition that the progenitors of the Campine were introduced into Flanders (northern France and Belgium), about the eighth century by the agents of Charlemagne. As king of the Franks and Emperor of Rome, Europe was a conquest to him, and it is recorded that he zealously endeavored to promote agriculture and required the farmers to keep a certain number of chickens, the millers to keep a certain number of ducks, and he required that certain kinds of fruit trees be planted. One so keen about increasing and improving the productions of his subjects may have sought to have an especial kind of chickens propagated, even introducing them from some foreign country.

That at one time or another the race came from the shores of the Mediterranean, there seems to be little doubt. But the origin of ancient breeds we cannot know with certainty. The lapse of time and lack of records make it impossible to trace their wanderings. So the exact origin of the ancient Campine is hidden in the past. But coming to more modern times, we have the Friesland fowl of the Netherlands, Het Friesche Hoen, formerly Friesche Pel.

Writing of this fowl, the late Louis Vander Snickt says: "The Friesland is extraordinary homogeneous," and it is "the mother race of all these egg-laying breeds with slate colored legs and white ear lobes." Of this stock the Hamburg was the first to be bred to feather, indeed, the occasional bringing together of Spangled Hamburgs in the village inns of

Yorkshire and Lancashire, England, about the middle of the eighteenth century, marks the beginning of poultry exhibitions.

The first selective work with the Campines was be-

In the summer of 1911, we were the guest of Monsieur and Madam A. F. Van Schelle, Papenvoort-par-Hoogstraten, Belgium. Hoogstraten lies east of Antwerp and is situated in that sandy plain near the Dutch frontier, where the Campine fowl is indigenous. At the time of that visit it was our privilege to visit the homes of a number of Belgian peasants and inspect their flocks of poultry. Both Golden and Silver Campines were to be seen, also a great deal of Leghorn blood was evident—"Italians" the Leghorns are called in Europe. So many Campines were being bought up by French buyers that Leghorns were used to an alarming extent to repopulate the poultry yards. The house in the above picture, which is a farm house in the Campine country in Belgium, was largely built out of poultry profits. It is a more prosperous appearing home than was to be seen before poultry culture became an industry in the Campine district. The lower picture shows a straw poultry house in the Campine country.—F. L. Platt

gun about 1865 by a Mr. Van Horn. He was station master of St. Lierre at Turnhout, Belgium, and made a hobby of Campines, for thirty years breeding and improving them. He gave the peasants eggs and often his best cocks and even his pullets, thus improving their stock from a breeder's viewpoint.

The Campine takes its name from the sandy zone of La Campine in which it is bred. Its sister breed, the Braekel, is grown on the rich and fertile, loamy soil of southern Belgium. Louis Vander Snickt, whose boyhood home was at Grammont, was the champion of the Braekel. Toward the end of the sixties he became a great fancier, and with the influx of show stock from England, on which considerable money was to be made, he sent his Braekels into the country to isolated farms, where they were kept pure. Having become director of the Zoological Gardens of Ghent, from 1871-74, he ordered their eggs for distribution.

From 1876-81 there were exhibited some superb Braekel hens, "well-shaped, well-barred, and at the same time very strong and large." At that time, however, no distinction was made in the show room between the Braekel and the Campine, and they were put down as large and small specimens of one and the same breed.

After a lull of a few seasons the Belgian fancy was re-awakened by poultry lovers in Antwerp, who formed the society, "Avicultura." The first exposition took place at Bardo in May, 1884. Situated in the north and on the

Fig. 1—A farm yard Braekel hen imported from Belgium to Wales by the Rev. E. Lewis Jones.

border of the sandy plains of La Campine, Antwerp fanciers had the Campine close under their range of observation, and the classification of their new show was opened with separate classes for Golden and Silver Campines, which were followed with classes for Golden and Silver Braekels.

The last of August, 1884, the first International Poultry show was held. Leopold II, king of the Belgians, had said to the administration of the city of Ostend: "I wish Belgium to become the kitchengarden of London." To increase the interest in the poultry of the "kitchen-

garden," the authorities at Ostend entrusted to Louis Vander Snickt the organization of a great international poultry show. In opening the classes, he did not miss the opportunity to make places for both Braekels and Campines. Thus is fixed the time when a distinction was made between the Campine and Braekel families by both the friends of the Braekel and by the Campin-

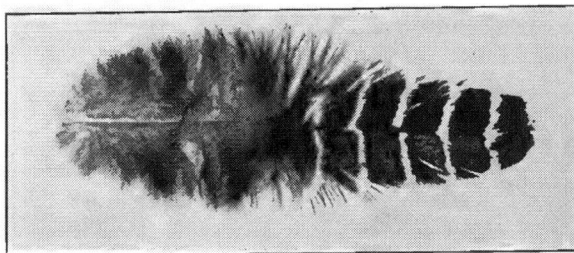

Fig. 2—Back feather from the third prize Silver Campine cockerel, shown by Capt. Max de Bathe, of Reading, England, at the Madison Square Garden, New York, Show of January, 1913.

ists of Antwerp and the north. In subsequent years, with the two breeds competing for superiority, rivalry flourished, and at Antwerp the Braekel was stricken out of the classification.

Color Agitation

At the beginning of the fowl's progress in the show room, the color pattern of the Campine-Braekel was not well established, nor the barring definite and clear cut. Fig. 1 illustrates a Braekel hen, such as may be seen today in the farm yards of the peasants in the Alost district of old Flanders. Such must have been the color of the females when they were first exhibited. In that early time the points for the Belgian breeds had not been specified and certain persons insisted that the Braekel female was a flower-colored bird and should not be barred, but selective breeding for bars prevailed in the yards of the fanciers.

The chief color agitation, however, has been about the plumage of the Campine males, and on this question there has been a great deal of controversy and no little excitement. At the start the Belgian judges preferred cocks almost white with black tails. Later, the barred breast and body came into fashion, while the hackle and saddle were still described as white "without blemish." This is the Belgian type of Campine and Braekel males today.

Already at Antwerp, in 1888, a cock of the present English type was shown, but he was not received with enthusiasm. "Why change the livery of the Campine?" wrote one of the critics of this bird. "Let us keep our old white Campine cock like his brothers, the Friesland and the Silver Penciled Hamburg." However, this plumage pattern, which in effect did not differ from that of the hen, was fostered by a few and bred in a Rose Comb Silver Campine variety. When in Europe some years later, Dr. H. P. Clarke, of Indianapolis, was attracted to these R. C. Campines, and his comments on them in "The Book of the Hamburgs" are as follows: "The hen feathering would not appeal to some tastes perhaps. I have talked with French and Belgian breeders who did not favor it. But to me it seems a positive attraction as well as an advantage. Both sexes being practically alike, there are no 'double mating' problems. The breeder knows exactly what to count on and so can secure more definite results and higher excellence generally, which fact is well illustrated in the case of the old Lancashire Mooney, a hen-feathered fowl whose perfection in spangling has never since been equaled."

A New Type is Introduced

In 1904 a male similar to the above, an all-barred cockerel, save the neck hackle, made its appearance in the English fancy. He was a Single Comb Silver Braekel, hatched from a sitting of eggs from Oscar Thomaes, of Renaix, Belgium. Renaix is in the south of Belgium and Braekels, not Campines, are everywhere kept in the surrounding country. The bird was first exhibited at Kendel, where he failed to attract attention. He was there purchased by a Mr. Wilson, who later showed him at the Grand International Show at the Alexandra Palace, and there he was awarded first prize and cup. The following year the same fancier exhibited the bird and some of his sons and won right along the line.

It was a sensational period for the Campine in England. Interest in the Belgian type had been at its height in 1902, and had already begun to wane. Fanciers were giving up and shows suffered. Then a new impetus was given; the English Campine Club adopted the new type and it thereupon became invincible in the show room.

In America the first Belgian Campines were received by Arthur D. Murphy, of Maine, in the year 1893. The breed was admitted to the Standard at the revision in Chicago during the World's Fair, 1893, and appeared in the edition of 1894. At this time J. H. Drevenstedt took an interest in the fowl, importing some from Belgium. An effort was made to push the fowl into popularity; it was heralded as the "every day layer" and the "300-egg-hen," but it failed to attract the fanciers; instead, its light flickered out, and at the next revision of the Standard the Campine was dropped from the lists of breeds.

The new English type of Silver Campine was imported by M. R. Jacobus, of Ridgefield, New Jersey, in 1907. At first the females, with their imperfect, mossy barring, and the males, with their unrefined combs, reddish-white lobes and perpendicular, scantily furnished tails, did not attract favorable attention at the New York and Boston Shows. But, when at the first showing of Campine eggs at Boston, January, 1910, the Leghorn eggs were defeated, the Campines began to advance in popular favor. Again in 1911, they won first, also in 1912 and 1913, at the last Boston Show there being no eggs entered against them.

Recently the color and style of the birds have been much improved. It is marvelous how superior in quality the winning Silver Campines have been at the New York Show the past two seasons, and at Boston and Philadelphia the past season. Of course, English-bred birds were in the foreground at these shows. Among the most successful producers whom we have known, are the leading Campinists of England. They are geniuses in poultry breeding. In 1911 when in England, we remarked to the president and the secretary of the English Campine Club that the combs of their birds must be brought down in order that imported stock might appeal more to Americans, and already the choice birds that England is exporting are models in this respect. A judge of prominence in Ohio, remarked to us: "The tails of the males are too high and there are not sufficient coverts to hold them down," but while his criticism was still heard, there was to be seen in the New York Show, December, 1912, the first prize Silver cockerel with graceful back line and sweeping tail. (See Mr. Sewell's photo of this bird, owned by Manhattan Farms, Brighton, N. Y., on page 7.)

Evolution of Type

From 1910 to 1914 has been a period of change for the Campine. Step by step the quality is advancing. As these steps of progress are set down, and inquiries regarding the effect of each change and the cause for it are made, the winning type of the present is better understood and more appreciated.

At the start Braekel hens often won in the Campine classes because of their more generous size. Now, size in a Campine is not the feature that recommends it to us. Mr. Vander Snickt pointed out that the preference should "be given to the smallest hens laying eggs of

Fig. 3——This cut was made from an unretouched photograph of the first Silver Campine pullet at New York, 1911. She was imported from England and shown by M. R. Jacobus, Box 3, Ridgefield, N. J.

75 grains." Such a bird matures more rapidly than a big, heavier boned one, and as a pullet, reaches the laying period first; she is naturally the more active, and with activity is closely associated productiveness.

In the Standard that was recently drawn up by the Standard committee of the American Campine Club, the following weights are specified: Cock, 6 pounds; cockerel, 5 pounds; hen, 4 pounds; pullet, 3½ pounds. The winners at the recent Club Show in New York were about these weights, with the exception of the first prize pullet, which was heavier. The Campine is a moderately tight-feathered and solid-bodied bird, and for its size is rather heavy, therefore, as one views them from the aisles the birds are somewhat deceiving about their weights.

It is the English-type Campine that has been accepted in America. While the English Campine is of Belgian Braekel extraction, it must be plain that the English have developed a race of their own, distinct not only in color, but in type. Americans are endeavoring to interpret the ideals of the English Campinists. The typical English Campines do not display the short legs of the Belgian Braekel, neither are they so thick through the shoulders, so heavy behind, or so big in bone. The Braekels in Belgium are somewhat of a two-purpose fowl, their eggs being shipped across the frontier to the French markets, while the poultry itself affords delicious "poulets" for the Brussels restaurants. Half a Braekel, lettuce salad, bread and beer form a favorite lunch in Brussels; and one restaurant that we patronized received on a standing order, 125 Braekels a day.

The Braekels, as we have seen them in Belgium in the farm yards of the peasantry, are broad and flat across the cape, with heavy shoulders and are moderately short and thick in shanks. The posterior section is well developed, indeed, rather heavy in some specimens.

Fig. 3 was made from an unretouched photo of an English-bred Silver Campine pullet, which was imported, and won first at the Madison Square Garden Show a year ago. She was shown by M. R. Jacobus, Ridgefield, N. J. You will note her apparent alertness and ready action, with which is accompanied a rather racy station. All this is typically Campine, the little Belgian Campines of the sandy plains having these characteristics. The shoulders of this pullet are not heavy, and behind she is neat like a Leghorn, rather than inclined to bag like a Dorking.

In the American Club Standard from which we take the liberty of quoting, the thighs and shanks are described as "rather long and slender," and the back of the female is described as "not too broad at shoulders, somewhat rounded across cape." It is easy to understand how a bird of this type could be too large and too coarse to be good.

As the Buff Leghorn male was elevated from the heavy, squatty type to the spirited Leghorn type of today, so selective breeding is being carried on to raise the Campine male to a good station. Big, tall, heavy birds, however, would resemble Minorcas, and the Campine should never be so coarse in bone or in the shanks so heavily muscular that they are not round like a lead pencil and the scales neat and finely laid on. Of all the defects, none should be more heavily penalized than rough shanks or signs of scabbiness. In the fine blue shanks a yellowish powdery crust under the scales, due to the scaly-leg mite, is most unsightly.

When a Campine is Judged

The legs are seen before you take the bird from the coop, and before he is shaped up. They are an important section; they are the foundation on which the chicken stands. In shaping up the chicken, it is desirable to give him the benefit of every point. Campine males are inclined to be a little sharp at the juncture of back and tail, and high in tail, so I gather the saddle hangers in my hand, and as the bird steps away I pull them over the tail and press the tail down. The longer the saddle feathers are the better. If the tail is a square henny brush, with short sickles, devoid of lesser sickles and poorly sided up with coverts, you can not do much to improve the carriage and such a bird should not be placed in a strong class.

In discussing the various sections of the bird, we will start at the beginning, which is the head, as if we had taken a bird from the coop and begun to handle it. In Belgium a very large comb is considered both desirable and pretty. American fanciers have insisted on refining the appendage to what may be termed med-

ium size. In the female the comb should rise to the first point and then fall to one side, as in the Leghorn; but the male comb should differ from that of a Leghorn, in that the blade proceeds slightly below the horizontal, having a tendency to follow the back of the head, but not resting upon the head, as in the Minorca. Five points are desired.

The eyes are a very important section of the head. Red eyes are a serious defect. However, judges in the average show, to whose lot falls the Campine, are not inclined to pay a great deal of attention to eye color so long as the general character of the bird is good. This is to be regretted. It would be easy to breed beautifully colored Campines when stress is not laid on the color of the eyes. With the red eye of the English Silver Penciled Hamburg, the clear cut barring and beautiful color of the English Hamburg also asserts itself. The eye should approach black in color, the iris being "dark brown and the pupil black." The English Standard calls for the same, and the Belgian Standard reads: "Eye: Vetch (chick pea), that is to say, very dark, appearing black." There is an economic value in this dark eye. When the matter was before the club's standard committee and the discussion was whether red eyes should be an absolute disqualification, Mr. Jacobus remarked: "I bred a red eyed bird and he cost me between two and three thousand dollars. Not over 5 per cent of his pullets laid white-shelled eggs. We must produce better eggs than the Leghorn lays." Vander Snickt says: "The eye should be black * * * an expression of face almost like a 'negresse,' and this excess of black and bluish pigment on the face has unquestionably some connection with the quality of the egg." It may be well to add here that in judging Silver Campines, if some blue pigment is streaked in the comb, it should not be considered a defect or an indication of poor physical condition.

Ear-lobes are frequently defective in the males, almost solid red lobes being seen occasionally. However, when the red covers more than one-half of the lobes, the bird should be passed. The lobes should be white, but a tint of blue in those of the female should not be decidedly objectionable. The wattles should be medium size and nicely rounded, not long and folded. They are usually found good.

Color of Back Very Important

The most important color section of the bird is the back. In Fig. 2 is reproduced a feather that was plucked from the back of the third prize Silver cockerel at the last Madison Square Garden Show. The color of the feather—and of the Silver Campine plumage—is black, barred with white. No matter about the undercolor; that has been a bug-a-boo in the American fancy for forty years. Now, as new breeds come in, let us put them on the right basis for breeding, enabling the fancier to concentrate his efforts on the surface color, that part of the plumage which is at once seen and first appreciated. The more green lustre in the black of the surface, the better. Stripes of gray running through the black bars, or intermediate barring, as it is called, makes a mossy appearance, and clouds the clearness of the well-defined white bars snapping out vividly against the glossy, greenish black. This mossiness or intermediate barring is commonly found in the females. While the white bars are narrow, the plumage should not have a blackish appearance, for a clear cast is secured by each feather ending with a white bar. The barring of the back is naturally more or less V-shaped, in fact, judges should not cut for or insist on straight barring in the back of the male.

The more barring in the tail the better, up to a certain point. We should not give the preference to nicely barred main tail feathers that run gray, then white at the base, rather than to a moderately well-barred tail of sound color. The latter bird plainly has the greater strength of color and greater breeding value.

Strength of color in the wings is also important. Frequently the secondaries are nicely barred. Gray primaries when opened out are unsightly, and when clear cut barring is not to be found in the primaries, black with positive streaks and spots of white is much to be preferred to a gray, washy color, which is sure to fade and become more indefinite from year to year. When the white penciling in the back is too wide, the primaries are apt to be weak in color.

We have deferred reference to the hackle until now, for, upon observing the wings and turning the bird over to examine the throat and breast, we find that when the hackle is white the throat and upper breast barring is apt to fail, and what you have gained in hackle is offset in a defective throat plumage. In judging chickens, one must balance qualities. When the back penciling of white is not too wide and the wings are sound and the throat nicely barred, the specimen— a well barred one—will win and the judge will not expect the penciling to break off suddenly with the beginning of the hackle. Of course, a hackle in which the penciling runs heavy well up towards the head, presents a most unattractive extreme of color. Fig. 3 illustrates good body color, with a consequent amount of markings in the hackle—a permissible amount. From males with a few white-tipped feathers in the black, yet soundly barred, are to be bred females with the clearest hackles and sound body color.

Coming down to the breast, crescentic markings are often seen in cheap birds. When the hard surface breast feathers terminate and the fluff begins, the black is frequently grayish and the white not clear cut, but partaking somewhat of the black. In the really first grade specimens the barring here is as firm and strong as on the front of the breast.

The body in many specimens is nicely marked. In mating or judging, always remember that a great wealth of plumage in the hackle, saddle and tail of the male is most desirable. The foundation male of both the Silver and the Golden Campines were "henny" males, and the best breeders are now striving to produce males with cock-plumage and at the same time hold a plumage pattern and color which is identical with that of the female.

Campines in Belgium, England and America

A Short History of the Campine and its Sister Fowl the Braekel—The Braekel-Hamburg and Braekel-Campine Crosses — Their Utility and Fancy Qualities—They Are Layers of Large, Heavy, White-Shelled Eggs and their Flesh is White and Delicate, Hence it is Expected That they Will Please Those Who Breed For Market Eggs and Fowls—How to Mate—The Golden Campines—Campines in America in the Early Nineties

By F. L. Platt

THE Campine is a heavy layer of heavy eggs. It is a Belgian breed that upwards of six hundred years has been grown as the "farm chicken" by the peasants who live on the sandy plains of the district of La Campine, which is the largest county in Belgium, and includes that part north of Brussels and west of Antwerp. This sandy country is covered with a scrub growth of brush about knee high and natural food is scarce, so the Campine chickens must from necessity be good foragers—they must roam far in search of food and be quick to catch every form of bug life. Therefore they are an active race, and in breeds of poultry alertness and small size are associated together.

While the Campine in its native country covers a great deal of ground searching for food and is active afoot and good on the wing, it knows its master and is not afraid. Along about dusk when the birds congregate in the barn yard or come into the door yard, they are not easily

A winning Silver Braekel hen bred by A. Rombaut, Gand, Belgium. The tail of the Braekel is more perpendicular than that of the Belgian Campine. The Braekel is broader backed and it has the strong legs and muscular shoulders of the Minorca. The tail of the Belgian Campine is more horizontal and the birds more closely resemble the Hamburg.

frightened, but are friendly. When fitted for the show room, they are good posers, and are gentle and comfortable to handle.

The Campines are pretty birds, but it was not until about 1865 that any attention was paid to breeding them for feather and form. A Mr. VanHorn, who was station master of St. Lierre at Turnhout, Belgium, made a hobby of the Campines and during thirty consecutive years was engaged in breeding and improving the Campine breed. He gave the peasants eggs, often his best cocks and even his pullets, thus improving their stock from the fancier's viewpoint—making it more desirable and valuable.

It was this stock from La Campine that was imported into England and exported to America. They were admitted to the American Standard of Perfection, and appeared in the edition of 1894. The back description of the male called for a white saddle. These white-topped males were white in the wing bow and white in the wing bay. When these Silver Campines with white tops were shown at New York in the early nineties, M. R. Jacobus, who was then breeding Hamburgs, saw them and said: "Think I would touch those things—they are nothing but Hamburgs, and poor ones at that." That was in the days when the Hamburgs, with their marvelous barring, symmetrical carriage and perfection of detail, the Cochins with their accentuated feathering, their convex lines of beauty and their softness of plumage color, and other beautiful breeds of the fancier were high in popular favor. It was before the present day of high cost of living and the productiveness of the Campine failed to secure for it a permanent place in America. In England the fowl was more favorably received and enjoyed an initial boom. The Campine Club of England was formed in 1899 and in 1902 had a membership of 77. However, the call for stock

GROWING CHICKENS IN BELGIUM.

birds and eggs for hatching necessitated the wholesale importation of birds from Belgium and these imported birds failed to satisfy the fastidious English fanciers. Naturally the fowl failed to prove up and drifted out.

The New Campine

In England the revival of interest in the Campine dates back about five or six years, when the hen-feathered stock began to command attention. This new type was not received without strenuous objection from those who, having been fortunate enough to have some of the best stock, were faithful to the breed and championed the white top color of the males. However, the hen-feathered type of male prevailed.

When the new type came on in England it was received by a new set of breeders. In America there had been a void period between the departure of the old and the arrival of the new Campine. But in England, while some fanciers gave up, shows suffered and enthusiasm flagged, it was only temporarily. The Campines were at the height of their popularity in 1902 and then the decline began. The first hen-feathered Silver Campine male appeared in 1904 and with it a plumage more flattering to the eye was created and the depression was replaced by greater enthusiasm, competition

was stimulated by the keen desire to obtain the advanced type, and a new lease of life was given to the Campine fancy of Britain.

The new Campine, while in name a Campine, is in blood half Braekel. The first hen-feathered cock came from the yards of Oscar Thomaes, Renaix, Belgium. Renaix is in southeastern Belgium, near the French border and it is in this district that the Braekel chicken is grown. This cock was exported to England and there bred for the sake of the new fashion which it had set.

The Braekel contributed some good qualities to the new Campine. The Braekel in Belgium lays a larger egg than its sister, the Campine. It gave to the new Campine more meat qualities, for the Braekel is a delicious table bird and much larger than the industrious little Campine that one sees on the sandy plains of La Campine. One Sunday noon last July, the writer sat in a restaurant in Brussels with Louis Vander Snickt, the great Belgian poultry authority, who has since died, and he said: "There are 300 Braekels a day furnished to this restaurant. I know it to be so for I know the man who supplies them." He and I and his maid—for he was not well at the time and could not go about alone —were each served half a chicken, and the bill for each was a franc and 25 centimes, or about 25 cents.

This price is not less illustrative of the value of poultry meat in Belgium than it is of the value of other foods, the cost of production, the margin of profit, and the necessity for rigid economy. Belgium is a small country. This morning we took a map of Europe that measured two feet wide and 20 inches high—put our thumb on it and blotted out Belgium! It is the most densely populated country in Europe. To the square mile it has one-third more population than England yet it not only produces poultry meat and eggs enough for home consumption (and the Belgians are great consumers of poultry products) but it exports to England, France and Germany. F. L. Sewell has said of the Belgians that they are the greatest producers and the best rearers of poultry in the whole world.

The Braekels and the Malines are their great commercial breeds. Varieties of the latter correspond to our Plymouth Rocks and Brahmas in size, and are kept in the soft roaster-producing districts. The flesh of both breeds is white.

Campines and Braekels of Common Origin

The Braekel may be said to have been the backbone of the new Campine. Crossing has been easily possible and quite practical. Presumably the Campine and Braekel came from the same stock and environment has played the role of the breeder for the past six centuries. On the rich ground of that portion of Belgium of which the Braekel is a native, the birds do not need to forage far, and for countless generations have been well nourished. Consequently the Braekel is the larger and more docile race.

The Belgian Campine is a graceful bird, similar to the Hamburg and it has a low carried tail. The tail of the Braekel is more perpendicular and the bird is square across the shoulders, broader backed and fuller bodied. In color and feather markings it is identical with the Belgian Campine.

When one considers the Braekel's greater size and heavier egg, it is interesting to learn why the Campine was taken up first by English breeders. Fortune favored the latter. It was more within the range of observation, being bred near to Antwerp. Edward Brown, of London, whose letters to the poultry press led to the introduction of Campines into England, states that although he made several trips to Belgium prior to 1897, he did not see a Braekel until that year.

It was through the good efforts of M. R. Jacobus that America was saved from the burden of that hyphenated name, Campine-Braekel. When the tentative American Campine Club was formed in Buffalo, N. Y., in May, 1911, Madame Annie F. Van Schelle, of Belgium, was present, and she urged a descriptive name rather than a brief, commercial one. However, with both varieties acknowledged in our land, the early hatched and large pullets would in some instances be termed Braekels and the late hatched and runts as Campines.

Braekel-Hamburg Crossing

The generous size of the Braekels tempted breeders to cross them with Silver Penciled Hamburgs. From the standpoint of the Campine breeder it may be said

ON THE ROAD TO MARKET, BELGIUM

that the Hamburg is a small fowl, a layer of comparatively small eggs and a fowl inclined to colds, and that the crossing is undesirable for the sake of utility. From the standpoint of the Hamburg breeder, it may be said that the securing of distinct penciling in the Campine through Hamburg crossing, is taking an unfair advantage of the fanciers of penciled Hamburgs, who have labored so earnestly for so many years for the perfection of the plumage of their race. They may add that the Campine coming as a common fruit a few years ago, has had grafted upon it the beauty of feather that has come from years of selective breeding, and that it now blossoms competitively with the Hamburg. The fact remains that the present generation is long in cash and short on time, and it was not content to spend three quarters of a century breeding up the Campines when so short a route was open.

We expected to see in Belgium both Single and Rose Comb Campines, but there are no rose combed birds throughout the district on the farms of the peasants. However, R. C. Hamburgs and the Belgian S. C. Campines undoubtedly sprang from a common source. The plains of La Campine do not stop at the Dutch frontier, but the same sandy soil continues well up into Holland, the native country of the Hamburgs.

The apparent influences of the Hamburg crossing are deprecated by Campinists. At the 1911 meeting of the English Campine Club, the Rev. Sturgis spoke in behalf of the pure bred Braekel-Campine, and resolutions were passed to fix a standard weight of 5½ pounds for cocks and 4 pounds for hens.

Campinists seek to keep their fowls distinct from the Hamburgs. One of the serious defects of a Campine is a red eye which is standard

MARKET HAMPERS FOR LIVE CHICKENS, BELGIUM.

in Hamburgs, while in Campines the Standard calls for the iris to be dark brown and the pupil black.

As a first working basis the English Campine Club's Standard was accepted by the American Campine Club. The first of the "serious defects for which birds should be passed" is: "Even barring, i. e., the white being equal in width to the black." The Campine's black bars should be "three times the width of the ground color" or white. The Standard for the penciled Hamburgs reads: "White (with) parallel bars of greenish black." There is a general resemblance between the Silver Campines and Braekels of Belgium and the Silver Penciled Hamburgs, and it is possible and probable that they have common ancestors, but the English Campine Club, in 1908, speci-

Fig. A.—English hen feathered type of Campine.

Fig. B—Belgian type of Campine showing white top and flowing sickles.

fied a width for the black bar and this was done to make a definite, a positive standard for the English Campine and to separate it for all time to come from the Hamburg and its barring of equal width. Hamburg crossing never-the-less continues and at the last meeting of the English Club at the Crystal Palace, a recommendation was proposed to "keep to the herring-bone markings instead of the straight ring barring of the Hamburgs."

The black of the Campine bar should be greenish black—the more lustre the better. Perhaps, we shall never vie with the English in the production of greenish black. The English Black Orpingtons have a lustre not equaled by American bred birds, just as the deep green foliage of the trees and the green grass of England is not to be surpassed. It must be the climate. The English birds that have been shown in America have been marvels of richness of color. The secondary bar, that is the faint gray or brown pencil in the black bar is being eliminated. The green-velvet black with the pure white bar running across, as seen in the plumage of the Standard birds is most attractive.

There is something especially delicate and pretty about a Campine pullet. We are fond of their big, dark eyes, silvery white hackles, and black and white colored plumage. Their clean and fine boned shanks are in harmony with the nice proportions of body and ease of

carriage and the blue shank color matches well with the plumage.

In the males of this new English type the feathering has been like that of the females, the long saddle hangers and flowing sickles being absent. With the barred back, wing bow and wing bay in the males, it was necessary to breed hen feathered males and make them standard. It has been the aim to breed as much cock plumage, i. e., as long feathers in the saddle and as much tail coverings on the tail, as possible. It is now expected that the two main sickle feathers should extend beyond the main tail feathers. One thing common to all hen-feathered males is their high tail, and it has been a defect in the Campines. See Fig. A. What beautiful tails, however, may be had in the English type Silver Campine males is illustrated in the cockerel shown on page 46. This was the 1st cockerel at the Madison Square Garden Show, December, 1913.

After a sojourn of several months in Europe, in 1911, in which time he visited Germany, France, Belgium, Holland and England, Artist A. O. Schilling returned to America partial to the original Belgian type, that is, he preferred the birds having long white saddle hangers, white shoulder on the wings, etc. See Fig. B. At the Pittsburg Show that winter he said to us: "I prefer the silvery-white tops. I would consider the silver-topped male the more beautiful of the two, in form especially. Nature didn't intend the male to be colored and feathered like the female. The hen feathered male is higher in tail and less symmetrical. He came as a sport originally and I object to his femininity." Since that time Mr. Schilling has become one of the most enthusiastic admirers of the English type, and has been called upon to place the awards in this variety at the Chicago Show.

Mating Silver Campines

Some of the English type males come with a few white saddle feathers. Such birds are often faked for show, the white feathers being plucked. Such a cockerel usually has a clear white hackle, and according to the English view, should be bred for the production of beautiful pullets. In breeding, Rev. E. Lewis Jones, secretary of the English Campine Club, gave us the following directions:

"For cockerels mate a male with excellent barring and plenty of sheen, to quite dark colored hens, free from the secondary bar. For pullets mate a male with a regular, even barring, the white bar being nearly as wide as the black, and a bird showing some white feathers in saddle. He should be mated to Standard colored females."

Golden Campines

This is the most distinctive variety that has been seen in America in a decade. It has a black and golden-bay bar—a combination that no American breeder, though he try ever so hard, had been able to make.

Golden barred Rocks had been attempted for years, but only a golden and white barring could be produced. There is something mysterious about the history of this variety of the Campines in England. It was recognized by the Poultry Club Standard before a single specimen had ever been produced. The English type Golden Campine was also pictured and painted before its arrival. Fact is: The variety is of very recent origin—the first true type birds being shown in England and America the same season—1911. It is a beautiful fowl, if anything larger and sturdier than the Silver variety; but with the exception of the strain of M.R. Jacobus, is more inclined to lay tinted eggs than is the Silver Campine.

There can be no doubt that the Campines have had a boom in the United States. This is partly due to their unique features, also to unusual publicity, and possibly to the fact that they were "imported." The great demand has resulted in wholesale importing. When the rage first started, Rev. Jones wrote us: "Americans are so keen now buying Campines that all sorts of rubbish is being sent out at prices from $50 upward." Let us say here in all fairness to our personal friends of the English fancy, and yet in equal fairness to Americans, that imported Campines do not stand up in our climate as well as birds grown in our climate. Had it not been for the tremendous vigor of the breed's early promoters, it is quite possible that the English Campine would have "died a borning" in America. Fertility was low, mortality high, while the imported stock was subject to roup. Geo. Urban, Jr., first president of the American Campine Club, in a letter to one of his customers wrote: "We think all the Campine needs is a few years of American breeding as all our trouble has been with imported Silvers, but they are getting acclimated now to their general improvement."

In Belgium the demand for the common stock was equally great in the years 1910, 1911 and 1912. There tne stock of the peasants in both the districts of Flanders, where the Braekel is bred, and the Campine country was eagerly purchased and exported for utility purposes. In the summer of 1911, Madame Van Schelle introduced us to the secretary of the Belgian Campine Club, who told us of a French buyer who was coming into the Campine country and who had forewarned him that he wished to purchase 2,000 pullets. How in the world he could find that many is more than we know, as the Leghorn is already making inroads on the native egg laying fowls of Belgium.

Campines and Braekels, however, are being continually exported to France and England, also Switzerland and the egg producing section of northern Italy. Belgium is losing her fine fowls through extensive exportations. Rev. Jones states that in 1910 he was actually unable to buy a shipment of pullets in all Belgium, as the French buyers had preceded him.

There is no doubt about the utility qualities of the fowls. They lay a white shelled, heavy egg. The shell is not as large as that of the Minorca, but the substance is weighty. At the Boston Show of 1911, eggs from Mr. Jacobus' Silver Campines won the first prize for the "best dozen of white shelled eggs," also first for the "whitest dozen." It was the first time in fifteen years that the Leghorn eggs failed to win these best prizes. The Campine eggs repeated this winning at the Boston Show of January, 1912, and in addition won first for the "handsomest display." There were twelve dozen Campine eggs in the form of a great star which won this prize. As great layers, the claim of 300 eggs a year per hen has been made for them. However, an egg every day for three hundred days, with a vacation of sixty-five days, may appear reasonable to the city man who has to work like the mischief and whose vacation in summer barely covers a fort-night, but records of 300 eggs per annum or even 250 for a flock "sweeps all the glory and practical utility out of sight," and we trust that no one will anticipate his profits on this basis of production.

When the Campines first attracted attention in America the extravagant 300-egg assertion was made. One of the critics of this claim wrote an article which appeared in R. P. J. for April, 1894, and what he said is pertinent now.

"I am glad our people have the enterprise to get men interested in things new and good, to get us out of the ruts and teach us that this is a new era and though grandpa may have been a good man, in every respect, our thoughts, methods, happiness and ideals call for something never dreamed of in the good old times.

"However, any intelligent breeder knows that no hen yet invented has made such a record in the States. The people of America would be glad to own such prolific stock. Half the fowls now kept would then do the work. Every one is anxious to own the best and should a better fowl be produced than our best now at hand, merit will win and sales will be easily made. That is all I can see in a big record—future sales at enormous prices."

Why America Did Not Accept the Belgian Type

Mr. Jacobus Was the First to Import English Type Campines to America — He Also Experimented With Belgian Stock in His New Jersey Climate—The Credit for Improving the Belgian Stock to Meet the Requirements of England and America Belongs to the English

By M. R. Jacobus, Ridgefield, New Jersey

DURING the years 1911, 1912 and 1913 there appeared in the foreign poultry papers, as well as the poultry press of this country, many articles on the Campines. In articles that refer to the type of the breed, some writers advocate the English type, while other writers advocate the Belgian type. From the statements in some of these articles, it is very evident that the Belgian breeders are very much disappointed because the Belgian type of Campines has not been accepted, not only by the English Campine Club, but also by the American Campine Club. One Belgian writer has gone so far as to practically accuse the English Campine Club or its members of having taken steps to have the English Standard admitted into America. This statement I feel is not only very unfair to the English Campine Club and its members, but also to the American Campine Club and its members.

Being the first American breeder to import the English type of Campines, I feel if the English had taken any steps or attempted to use any influence to have the English type accepted in America in preference to the Belgian type, I would have known of it. I must say that I cannot recall any effort on the part of any English breeders or breeder to induce me to accept or to have me use my influence to have the English Standard accepted in America in preference to the Belgian type of birds.

In addition to this I wish also to say that during my connection with the American Campine Club as secretary, I have never known of any effort on the part of the English Campine Club or its members to have the English Standard adopted by the American Campine Club.

As stated above, I feel that the statement that, "The English had taken steps to have their Standard admitted in America," is unfair to the American Campine Club and its members, as well as to the members of the English Campine Club. I view such a statement as being equivalent to saying that by efforts on the part of the English breeders the American Campine Club would have adopted the English Standard, even if the birds of this type had not been much better fitted for the conditions of this country, than the birds of the Belgian type were.

When I first brought the English type of Campines to America there were breeders advertising the Belgian Braekel. If the English used any influence in having the English type of Campine accepted in America, their

The most attractive plate of eggs at the Boston show, 1913, was shown by M. R. Jacobus. These eggs won first for being the largest and best dozen white eggs. Mr. Jacobus also won the best ten plates of white eggs. All of these were laid by his Campines that have been doing most of the winning and making a name as producers of white eggs at the big Boston shows during several years past. Mr. Jacobus has found that buyers are well impressed by his exhibits of eggs and that the big white eggs are doing a great deal to increase the popularity of the Campine.—F. L. Sewell.

influence was used by the fine type of birds they originally sent to this country. In making their original type of Campines, it was very evident that the English used a great deal of care, not only in the selection and production of well marked birds, but also in the selection and production of birds that laid large white eggs, which were far superior to any eggs that I have been able to secure from the Belgian birds.

Some eighteen or twenty years or more ago, Belgian Campines were sent to this country and exhibited at Madison Square Garden, New York City. Shortly after this they were admitted to the Standard of Perfection, this Standard calling for what was practically the Belgian type. As such a type did not appeal to the American fanciers and breeders, they shortly discontinued their breeding and then the Campines, which were in reality the Belgian type Campines, were dropped from the Standard of Perfection.

The Belgian Campines which were exhibited at Madison Square Garden some eighteen or twenty years or more ago, did not appeal to me, so of course I did not take them up. If all the Campines that came to this country had been of the Belgian type, I never would have made any effort to introduce them into this country even at the present day.

When I imported my first pair of English type Silver Campines from England, I had no idea of taking them up as a breed. I simply wanted this pair for cross breeding purposes. When I received this first pair I was very much surprised to find that they were much handsomer than the Belgian birds, which I had seen exhibited years before. Seeing at once the big difference from the Belgian type of Campines which had been sent to this country years previous and discarded by American breeders, I at once saw that they could be bred from a single mating and that by careful selection still handsomer birds could be produced.

While the markings and the fact that they could be bred from a single mating was attractive, I am ready to admit that it was the very large white eggs that this hen laid that impressed me most of all. I at once sent back into England for more Campines, as I saw there was a big future for this breed if properly handled.

After first exhibiting the English type of Campines in America I found that I was not creating a demand as fast as this worthy breed deserved. Knowing that the English type of Campines was the proper type for this country and knowing that it deserved to be extensively introduced throughout this country, I decided that in simply exhibiting these birds I was not doing half my duty to this type of birds. Knowing that their eggs were far superior to any heavy laying breeds, I decided to exhibit the eggs laid by this original type of English Campines, as well as exhibiting the birds.

After making such exhibits of eggs the fanciers and breeders began to take great interest in the Campines. The poultry papers paid great compliments to the exhibits of eggs laid by this breed. After this it was not long before there was a great demand for Campines. American breeders then started to import birds from abroad, not only from England, but also from Belgium.

If the American breeders who imported the Belgian type of birds had found this type to be the best fitted for America, I feel that some breeders of this Belgian type would have made a request of the American Campine Club that the Belgian Standard be adopted by the American Campine Club.

When the permanent organization of the American Campine Club was formed at Madison Square Garden, New York, December 21, 1911, every person present realized that the English Standard best fitted the requirements of this country, and for this reason the club decided to use the English Standard as a guide this year, and that the executive board draw up a new Standard to be presented at the next meeting of the club, to be held at the coming Madison Square Garden Show. When the vote was taken to decide if the club use the English Standard as a guide this year, there was not one vote in opposition to doing so.

Long before the meeting when it was decided to use the English Standard this year, some breeders who had imported Belgian birds had already procured males of the English type which they were crossing with the Belgian females, as they saw that this would be the first step towards improving such Belgian birds.

A few years ago in fairness to the Belgian type of birds, I imported thirty Belgian birds for comparison. Of course before importing these Belgian birds I really knew what the Belgian birds were, not so much from what I had seen years previous, but from some birds I would raise at times when the English type would revert to the original Belgian bird.

As I expected my English type of birds were far superior to these Belgian birds, and for this reason I have discarded my Belgian type birds, except a few I have reserved to show visitors to my yards the vast difference between the two types.

I also found that the Belgian females as a whole were not equal in egg qualities to the original English type, to say nothing of the poor markings of the Belgian birds as compared with the English type. After the above test one can understand why I have advised to kill all males that reverted to the Belgian type.

From what I have said in this article I do not wish my readers to feel that it is my opinion that the English type of Campines cannot be improved to make them still very much better for this country.

While I know there are improvements to be made over the English type of Campines better to fit them for conditions in America, I do not wish to be understood to mean that the English have not the best type of Campine for their country, for I feel breeders of Great Britain are aware of the type that best fills their requirements. Further I wish to say that I do not wish to be understood to believe that the Belgian people have not the best type of birds for Belgium. As these birds have been bred for centuries in Belgium, I feel that the small Belgian Campine of the plains of La Campine must be the type best fitted for that section of Belgium, and I also feel that the larger type or Braekel which are found on the more fertile plains of Belgium must be best fitted for their particular section.

I do not think it would be just to the Belgian people to expect them to adopt a type that is better fitted for some other country than it is for Belgium. I will also say that the Belgian people should not expect people of any other country to adopt the Belgian type of Campines after some other type has been proven to be much better fitted for that particular country, even if Belgium has types of its own that are best fitted for the conditions of the particular sections of Belgium in which they are found.

In addition to saying that I believe that England and Belgium each have the best type of Campines for their particular countries, I wish to give to the breeders of Belgium my thanks and the credit due them for preserving this breed for centuries and offering it to the world to be improved in such ways as will best fulfill the requirements of the country adopting this breed.

To the breeders of England belongs the credit of improving the Belgian birds to meet the requirements of their country. By taking the large Braekel and the small active Campine as they found them in Belgium and by careful selection and breeding and possibly by the infusion of other blood, they produced the original English type of Campine.

As England originally had a type of Campines that was better fitted for America than the Belgian type, the demand for birds from England has been very heavy not only for large numbers of breeders, but also for fine marked birds. In their efforts to meet this demand the English must be very careful and send to this country only such birds as have all the good qualities that were contained in the original type of English Campines. They must be careful and not sacrifice the egg qualities as contained in their original type of birds, even if they do not meet the demand for large numbers of breeding, or if they do not send as handsomely marked birds as some exhibitors desire.

What breeders of America want are birds that cannot be surpassed by any as egg producers. After this they want a strain that can be easily bred and look as handsome as possible, provided they do not sacrifice the egg qualities for fine markings.

The Campine Braekel—A Noted Belgian Race

Belgium the Home of the Campine-Braekel, The Bird With a Future as Well as a Past—The Two Hundred and Fifty Egg Hen Found Among the Campines—Remarkable Development of Egg Production in Belgian Fowls Due to Years of Careful Selection and Systematic Feeding and Handling

By Madame A. F. Van Schelle, Papenvoort-par Hoogstraeten, Belgium

THE world is looking for the 250 egg hen! Have we found her?

If we are to believe no less an authority than the late Lewis Wright, the Braekel-Campine is that gold mine. "Campines of really good stock are certainly amongst the very best layers known, many individual yields of 250 eggs being reported and these of wonderful size," (New Book of Poultry, Page 467.)

In these days we hear on every side such eulogies as, "the best layer on earth," and similar superlatives, so that we are forced to the logical conclusion that all breeds are best! However superficial such a statement may seem at first glance, there is more than a germ of truth underlying it, as by selection, and wise care, egg-laying qualities may be enhanced and transmitted up to an uncertain (?) degree, which the poultry world is trying to ascertain. (D. F. Laurie, Scientific Breeding and Heredity, page 5, "Is there a Limit?")

Now in America, when a thing is undertaken, it is not done by halves; perhaps in no other line of work has this been more marked than in poultry breeding. See what the State Agricultural Colleges have already accomplished in a short time. True, this is a branch where quicker returns may be made and consequent strides marked than in most lines of breeding, but America is destined to give an unequalled expansion to the poultry industry, provided she is not led away from sound principles by false prophets—who "boom" a breed solely for personal ends. Now just here let me make an application. If you had stood at shows, a silent listener to comments made by the masses on breeds unfamiliar to them, you would have had much food for reflection. You will agree that there is a class of men who, not understanding a man of another calibre, find the simplest way to dispose of him—is with the crushing word "crank." A like class in the poultry world not understanding utility breeding say, "mongrels," and feel their superior intelligence vindicated.

If you happened to examine the exhibit of Malines, you would probably have seen specimens that may be called scientifically "sports;" by the application of Mendelism these sports are fixed in varieties. What you have bred is in Mendel terms, a "Heterozygote," and the average breeder kills him as a mongrel—his goose that laid the golden egg. Mr. Laurie in his paper on "Scientific Breeding and Heredity; Research in Mendelism," says, "The enlightened breeder will cherish everyone of these colored "sports" (Heterozygotes), and, with all his breeding and feeding arts, mate them for the production of strains of pure dominants and pure recessives; and he can keep his impure dominants as a reserve strain. When he arrives at this point, he will at any rate have for the first time pure White Leghorns. "Here we see nature inviting us to give the finishing touches in perfecting our strains." I should advise every serious reader to study this pamphlet and to use it as his vade mecum. The day of "the chance success" in poultry breeding comes to most of us one day. But how many breeders are able to keep up to that standard once success has knocked at his door? Simply because they breed blindly they must fail, and then having a reputation, they try to keep it up by unjustified advertising, with a result of throwing opprobrium on serious patient breeders. It was Barnum, I believe, who said that the American public liked to be duped. It would seem that this is not altogether foreign to the poultry public. How much better it would be that we should work together shoulder to shoulder, trying to find out the truth of things, the reason why, and when we fail, ask ourselves Why?

POULTRY HOUSE ON BELGIAN FARM OF MME. VAN SCHELLE

A close-up view of growing chicks on the sand of the Campine country, Belgium. The pine trees and scrub brush are also seen to advantage in this view. The poultry building is on the farm of Madam A. F. Van Schelle, Papenvoort-par-Hoogstraeten, Belgium. American Campinists owe a debt that has never been paid to Madam Van Schelle. At an expense of nearly $3,000, she brought teams of Belgian fowls to America in 1910, and exhibited the birds at Chicago and as far west as Kansas City. She did much to educate Americans in "Campineology," and while one of the best of the continental breeders, her tremendous expenditures in 1910 and again in 1912 have never brought even fair returns, for England alone has enjoyed the influx of American dollars. We are glad to be able to pay this little, tardy tribute in a public work of this kind. Breeders who are today reaping the whirlwind of Campine popularity, little know the tremendous efforts that were put forth by the pioneers.

Again Mr. Brown states, in regard to the qualities of the breeds which have attained pre-eminence, and in some cases held a prominent place in the egg and poultry production of Belgium for a very long period, two points in this connection that should be emphasized: "First, that whilst the external characteristics of the respective breeds have been kept in view, evolved probably as a result of natural conditions, productiveness has been the determining factor; and, second, the fact has been recognized that to secure prolificacy in respect to egg-production a small-sized body is essential. Hence we find all the laying breeds are small and the table breeds large."

In a far away country across the sea (The Netherlands) a quiet painstaking priest discovered by his patient observation and experimentation with peas in his garden, certain truths. Now the world speaks glibly of these principles that he discovered in the laws of breeding, and heralds them as the Mendel Law.

"Belgians possess a great knowledge as to the science of breeding but refuse to reveal it. They are said to have known and practiced Mendel's Law for centuries." (Edward Brown in The Poultry Industry of Belgium.)

The same authority states "that the claims made that for more than a thousand years poultry have been bred and produced on what may be termed industrial lines; that is, systematically and for food production. As far back as 1054 the people of Brussels were called "Kiekefretters" (Chicken eaters). In going back to the old records in the time of Charlemagne in the eighth century one finds that the millers were obliged to keep ducks and the farmers poultry as they had to pay tribute in ducks and fowls to their land or over lord."

All of which goes to prove that in a small densely populated country with an area of 11,373 square miles, about one-fifth of the state of Illinois, and with a population of between seven and eight million inhabitants, the struggle for existence is keen. The Belgian is known the world over for his industry and thrift, and nowhere has he shown this to a greater degree than in breeding, especially in the smaller animals and birds. Consequently it is not surprising that he has made strides along industrial lines. It could hardly be otherwise. He has a message for you, American breeders. Are you ready to accept it and the hen that has made good around the world? I have come to you not only with this message; I have not come empty handed, but with a gift in each hand. In the one, the Braekel-Campine to fill your egg baskets; in the other, the Malines, the poor man's friend and support. Why should you not profit as other nations have done and do from this legacy that is proffered you? For these are hens not only with a past, but with a present and with a future. They are yours for the taking.

Five hundred years of lineage establishes an acknowledged aristocracy in beast as well as in man, for it is said, that it takes seven generations to make a gentleman.

Perhaps some skeptic would say that is sufficient time to fix sterility. Be that as it may, the Braekel-Campine for whom this claim is made continues to fill the poultryman's egg basket with large size eggs, and in his own country, she is called by the peasants who disdain trap-nests and modern paraphernalia, as "Doed Legger" or (Death-layer), as they claim that if improperly fed she will go on laying even when she is obliged to use up her substance to do this.

Egg Laying Records of Campines

	Jan.	Feb.	Mar.	Apr.	May	June	July	Aug.	Sept.	Oct.	Egg.
1907				20	30	22	24	2	27	21	146
1908	21	22	26	26	29	17	22	20	29	17	229
1909	14	18	23	24	24	18	25	16	8	9	179
1910	16										16
											570

"From January first '08, to January first, '09, hen No. 1 laid 229 eggs, hen No. 2 laid 226; they stopped laying October 30th, then in their full moult. Hen No. 2 began laying again January eighth, '09, this is their second year; this trio, being two years old last July. In their pullet year No. 1 laid 50 eggs in 53 days, No. 2 laid 35 eggs in 43 days, following the arrival of after an ocean voyage of 21 days. Breeding pen No. 3 with 7 pullets domestic stock, breeding pen No. 4 seven pullets domestic stock, the 14 pullets average 209 eggs per year.

Mr. Kennedy says in his circular, "When I say large white eggs I mean eggs averaging 27 to 30 oz. or over to the dozen, and by lots of them I mean flocks which will average 175 to 200 eggs each in 365 consecutive days. 'The hen that lays is the hen that pays,' quite true, but I wish to add that the hen that lays large white eggs and lots of them, pays better."

A lady in California who has bred Campines for many years writes under date of February 12th, that in July at the age of four months and four days, two pullets began to lay; after moulting began to lay again in November and December. They laid each five eggs one week, six the alternate week. March 12th they were a year old. Out of 17 pullets these were the two best layers. This was a private letter in which she also signals an advantage she finds in the Braekel-Campines, that they finish the moult in 2½ to 3 months against something like 4 months for Leghorns that wait for the sun before beginning to lay again, while the Braekel-Campines lose no time, but after 8 days' rest begin again. So much for an experience in California.

Record of Weight of Eggs

Mr. Fred L. Kimmey's record of the weight of the eggs laid by the Braekel-Campine hens and pullets exhibited at Kansas City and Chicago Shows recently is 32½ ounces to the dozen, an average of 2.7 per egg, or over three-fourths of an ounce over the two ounce market standard.

Valuable As Broilers

The by-products of this breed are turned to good advantage, as superfluous cockerels are considered the best breed for milk chickens. The reasons why are not difficult to see: Being very precocious the sex is distinguished at an early date. The comb is developed before they are in feather, and they crow at a little over three weeks of age. At eight weeks they should weigh eight to ten ounces and bring 40 cents apiece. At three months they are worth hardly 15 cents.

Beautiful As Exhibition Fowl

Very few will differ from the statement that the Braekel-Campine is a thing of beauty whether you take him in his Belgian Standard dress, appearing (1) on the green fields (at a distance) almost like a Yokohoma with shortened tail, really like a painted bird; or in his English garb, barred from breast to end of tail like his consort, with only one exception—a clean white neck hackle or cape. There is an elegance and finish about these birds that appeal to anyone who is appreciative of the beautiful.

One word of warning. Many of you know the history of the Braekel-Campine in England. The words of advice, of no less an authority than the Rev. E. Lewis Jones, to whom the Braekel-Campine owes largely her popularity in England, after a visit to Belgium solely to study this breed in its native country, cannot come amiss. "After a close study of the two breeds, I have come to the conclusion that it would have been better if Braekels only had been imported from the first, and for the future, I would advise the club to stick to the Braekel. I have said the Campine is better marked, and our judges will, for a time at least, have to decide whether markings as in Campines

or size as in Braekels is to win. The Braekel is sufficiently large to satisfy those who ask for a big bird. The Belgian fancy has the same difficulty rejudging separately. "Where Braekels and Campines are not classified, some fanciers told me it was their intention to draw up a separate standard. This I certainly deprecate, and as far as I can see, we are not likely to be troubled with it, as in a season or two the large sized Braekel would be equal to the Campine in markings, and will then win every time on size."

It is perhaps not a safe thing to prophesy, but please remember in time to come that from the beginning I have told you this is the coming bird in popularity in America.

All the world knows and appreciates a fresh egg.

Campines in Belgium, Holland, England and America

In Holland, Belgium, Parts of France and England, the Traveler Finds Penciled Fowls — The Campines Represent the Most Perfected Type of Dark Penciling—The Campine is a Member of a Great Family of Penciled Fowls —Americans Are Keen for Type — Combs Must be Refined and Pure Colored Earlobes Bred

By C. S. Theo. Van Gink, Amsterdam, Holland

THOSE who have watched the phenomenal progress of the Campine in the last couple of years must often have wondered why such a fine colored fowl as the Campine did not become popular long before this. It seems, however, that the few really well marked birds which came every season amongst all the youngsters, discouraged the greater part of those that took up the breed. However, since the modern males, those with the hen-colored plumage have been used exclusively, the color of the Campine has improved wonderfully, while the number of poorly penciled youngsters is far smaller.

A little history of the Campine will not be out of place and might explain a few things. Continental authorities who have studied the history of poultry in its earlier and later state, came to a conclusion, which they based upon notes that appeared in old books, that in the 15th century Dutch sailors quite often took fowls along and brought other ones back with them on their trips to the Orient. They did likewise with other birds and animals, which were sold here in Holland and went from here to Belgium, Germany and France, some even as far as Russia. Among the fowls they brought along with them (some claim they came from Persia) were white and buff chickens with crescent shaped markings, quite different from the markings found on domestic poultry over here at that time. From Holland they gradually went to the surrounding countries and at last also to England, and in each country they adapted themselves slowly but surely to the local climate and conditions. Some came bearded like the Dutch and the Thuringian owl bearded fowls, some became crested and bearded like the Brabantines, some furthermore became featherfooted like the laced Siberian fowls. I do not mention the Polish fowls because they were most probably imported also from Persia by the Italians but at a much earlier date. Every climate had its own influence, for instance under the mild conditions in England they

developed enormous combs for which the Redcaps are known now.

The above mentioned breeds all belong to the laced or spangled races, while the Campines belong to the penciled races, and as such are much closer related to the original color.

Those who are acquainted with the territory north of La Bresse, covering everything west of the Rhine, covering the Rhine-province, part of France, Belgium, Holland and the provinces East Friesland and Oldenburg in the northwestern part of Germany, will notice that this whole territory is full of penciled birds, light penciled in the southern part of it, gradually getting darker in color to the border of Holland and Belgium; and after that decreasing in quality of markings and becoming lighter in plumage until at the northern part of the territory in East Friesland and Oldenburg, where the penciling is again as light and imperfect as around the city of Bresse. The silver penciled Bresse fowls are single combed fowls, somewhat resembling the Silver Penciled Hamburgs in shape. The male is marked like the Hamburg male of that color, the female being penciled though very coarse, breast and the fluffy part hardly showing any penciling at all. We might term this the crude form of light penciling. North of this we find the Braekels, being dark, the white being almost gray between the bars. This may be called the crude form of dark penciling. In the territory adjacent to where the Braekels are found, we come across the Campines, whose territory is right on the border of Holland, and they represent the perfected type of dark penciling. Just a couple of hours farther north we come amongst the Chamish Fowls, only differing from the Campines by their eyes, which must be orange; then in the heart of Holland we have the Hamburgs as samples of the perfect light penciling. In Dutch Friesland we find the Frisian fowls which look like single comb Hamburgs, while in East or German Friesland we find the East Frisian penciled fowls, which are again like the above described penciled Bresse fowls, however a little smaller in size and longer in body, both belonging to the light penciled class.

This is in short the history of the Campine fowl which shows that it is one of the members of that family of penciled fowls which differ from each other only in color and shape, on account of the fashion and local condition every one of these sub-breeds had to meet with, but which are all of the same make-up.

Campines are not very popular right now in Belgium, Holland and Germany because the breeders in their native location are hardy fowls, with a good egg production, that thrive well when even common care is taken of them. Those who are of the opinion that there is a great difference between Braekels and Campines in their native country are far mistaken, because I often found myself at a loss to distinguish them. When one reads through the two different Standards of the Braekels and the Campines, the difference is easy to see, but when in the show room, one cannot help but think, when one looks at the birds as they are entered in the different classes or rather under the different names, that some Braekels surely do look more like

The ideal Silver Campine male and female of the Utility Poultry Standard, published by the "V. P. N." Utility Poultry Association of Holland.—C. S. Theo. VanGink.

these countries stick to the white topped males. But let us say that this brings with it the mussy penciling in the females. There are, however, a handful of breeders that have taken up the hen-colored types of males and cross them with their females to improve their strain. In Belgium they fill the classes pretty well. Besides the penciled varieties one sees in Belgium once in a while pure white and pure black Campines, as well as unicolored blues with black hackle and saddle in the males and a dark neck in the females. The Campines of these three colors often lack the dark eye, but it would not be hard to get it. Furthermore one finds the short legged Campines, which look like the Scottish Dumpies or Creepers.

Where in America and England only two distinct penciled varieties are known, there is a third penciled color to be found in Belgium and Holland. When crossing Silver and Golden Campines sometimes some chicks come reddish buff, but instead of the black penciling they have white penciling, the narrower the white the better the bird is. Only last week I saw a beautiful specimen of this color at the Utility Poultry Exposition at the Hague. Campines as they are found in

a Campine than some Campines do themselves. Several times I saw a big Campine hen entered in the Braekel class, the judge falling for it and giving the bird a first prize on account of its better penciling.

While at times hen-colored males cropped out in Belgium at several places, to the English breeders belongs the credit of having made use of this type and thus making the modern type of Campine males, which they made in comparatively few years with their fine knowledge of color breeding. A lot has been written and said about the supposed cross which was made between the Campine and the Hamburg and just as much has been denied and while the different breeders and authorities, as well as a bunch of born knockers were mixed in a red hot controversy with plenty of local color, the breeders went on and brought out their Campines better and better every year, while the breed pretty soon was enjoying a boom such as very few breeds ever before have had in England, with possibly the exception of the Black Wyandotte. The Campine as it is nowadays when in show condition is a treat to the eye and a first class show bird. I can hardly imagine anything more beautiful than a fine colored Campine, with its sharp edged black and white bars, standing on a pair of fine slate blue legs. Furthermore a fine Campine head is a great fancy point, their blood red comb, being in such sharp contrast with the bluish white earlobe. The dark eye gives the bird a more or less characteristic face.

For two season, 1911-1912 and 1912-1913, I had the good fortune to see the Campines at most of the big eastern shows in America, like the two New York Shows, Boston and Philadelphia. It was here that almost every star in the Campine world, home-bred or imported, made its debut. It was really a pleasure to see the big progress Campines had made both in quality and in the number of good birds. More especially I remember a Golden Campine cock, which had a wonderful penciled tail and saddle; the quantity of feather he carried was a most important point, too, because the ever decreasing length of the sickle feathers in hen-colored Campine males is a very important question which the breeders must keep well in mind and try to stop if not better.

It will surely be most interesting to watch the progress of the Campines in America. I fancy they will breed down their combs, which are rather beefy at this time, especially in cock birds, and take hold of the earlobes and wattles and try to make them better, but if anything, Americans will not stand for the high tails which some Campines are carrying around with them nowadays, and I believe I am right when I say, that the rather young cockerel which won the blue ribbon in the Silver cockerel class at Madison Square Garden, New York, Show, Dec., 1912, made quite a hit with the Campine people and he looked an easy winner long before the judge of the class had written down a single note. This bird which carried his tail in a pheasant-like way, with his long slender body, surely indicated the type of Campine that will find favor in the eyes of the American fancier. However, it may be said right here, that it is not the shape Campines have in their country, neither is it the shape they are striving for over here. However, Americans are so used to the wonderful outlines of their Leghorns that they have no use for shortbacked, hightailed fowls, for the simple

reason that they have been trying to get away from such a type in their Leghorns for more than two decades.

Personally I believe the Americans will produce a better shaped Campine than we will get over here, because their eyes are well trained when it comes to look for shape and symmetry.

This is one of the first things one must notice when coming to America. Every breeder and even the beginner is compelled to study shape, as he will have to enter birds as close as possible to the shape given in the Standard.

Right now Americans are much better judges of shape and outline than the Europeans, because over here they pay too much attention to color, with the exception probably of the Game fanciers.

By the time the 1915 edition of the American Standard of Perfection will be out, authorities and breeders will have settled the questions of color and shape, for instance they will have indicated the happy medium between a good breast and good neck; a couple of fine pictures will illustrate the standard and the breeders will know better than they ever did over here what is wanted both for shape and color. I do not know of any poultry association in the world which has such a good and strong influence upon the fancy as the A. P. A. May Campines benefit by it and may they long enjoy the popularity they have attained and take the place among the ranks of chickens, which they deserve by their beautiful appearance.

Note—As for the date of the first introduction of the modern type in English shows, Mr. Van Gink adds this interesting note:

"As far back as 1903 hen-colored Campines were known in England, because the Feathered World at that time published a color plate on which also a pair of hen-colored Campines appeared, while in June, 1908, the Poultry World, also of England, published a color plate of a very typical Silver Campine cockerel, showing to perfection the very narrow, clean-edged white penciling which is so much in demand right now. This male, which was perfectly hen-colored and showed even then the partly hen-feathered type, which was already prevailing among fine colored males at that time."

Exporting Eggs From the Braekel Country

The Old Jacobin Monks Made it a Point to See That the Peasants Had Productive Fowls—Today in One o the Markets of This District 30,000 Eggs are Marketed Every Tuesday—A Visit to the Great Egg Market of Audenarde—A Description of the Braekel Egg, Its Foundation and Soundness—The Advantage of the Large Egg

By F. L. Sewell

"IN THE early days of Belgium when the peasant gave one-tenth of all his produce to the Abbeys, the Jacobin Monks were the 'Ameliorators' and it was much to their advantage to see the peasant farmers in their district had the best and most productive races of fowls. These Jacobins were in communication with the Romans and looked well to it that the farmers contributing to their coffers had hens that could help to fill them."

The above explanation was given me when we were in company with the late Louis Vander Snickt one early autumn morning in 1905 on our way from Brussels to

Audenarde. As we passed out through Brabant, many active hens were out in the early dawn ranging over newly plowed fields. Farther out we came to Alost ("Land of hops") where the hens are all Braekels—many piles of hop poles could be seen.

As we passed through Sottegem, our traveling companion remarked, "Here the people are all good fools—they are very witty, they are poetic and make good actors." You will be interested to know every Tuesday they sell in the public market 30,000 eggs of 62 grammes * each. These come from the "Braekels" that live at the little farms dotting all over the meadowlands. The

* Sixty-two gramme eggs would weigh about 26 oz. to the dozen.

"Braekels," it will be remembered, are the low-land relatives of the Campines.

These low meadows in the remembrance of the older men were very much flooded in wet seasons, but now skirting nearly every field next to the row of trees bordering, runs a narrow ditch three to five feet in width, mirroring the blue of the sky or the green of the bordering hedge, the low branching trees or the rich grasses that hang trailing into their brink.

Soon after we left Sottegem our friend remarked, "Now we will be, all day, five hundred years behind— yes, all that you will see" and all but the fresh young pullets and crowing cockerels seemed to bear out his words. This was in the Valley of the Schelde.

At Audenarde we made our way to what proved one of the most interesting little poultry and egg markets we have visited. Punctuality and consideration for others were apparent even to a stranger.

At the far end of the open rectangle of marketers can be observed the dignified Gendarme who enforces order when necessary. While we looked on, order was perfect.

The photograph shows the poultry market at about eight-thirty o'clock. At precisely a quarter before nine, when the clock chimes the quarter hour, the buyers have their first look into the baskets. The marketers up to that instant are not allowed to open their baskets or to do any selling. From that moment the buyers pass rapidly from one basket to another examining its contents—purchasing the eggs. Twelve to fifteen thousand eggs were offered in the market that morning. The splendid sized, white eggs easily come up to the required 62 grammes each. There were also brown eggs in the market from the Malines and Huttegem.

The buyers arranged with the marketers to carry their eggs in the marketer's baskets over to the "Pomme de Orr" Inn opposite the left side of the large church that faces the square. In a large public room of this hotel the eggs were changed to the big hampers of the buyers that hold 1500 eggs each—the eggs arranged in layers with straw between and at sides.

The 62 gramme eggs brought 15 centimes (3 cents) each by the 1,000. These eggs are purchased to be sold to merchants over in France, who pay 20 centimes (four cents) each

The top picture shows the poultry market at Audenarde, Belgium. At a certain hour, the poultry buyers enter the open space, the peasants open their hampers and the poultry sale begins. The center picture shows a cargo of eggs in hampers ready to be carried acoss the frontier to the French markets. The bottom picture is typically Belgian. The peasants drive to market with dogs and ponies.

for them and the French merchant sells them for 25 centimes (five cents) and pays 6 francs per 100 kilo ($1.20 for 2.2 lbs.)

When all the eggs are well packed the large hampers are loaded on the big wagons and start on their journey over the road to Lille in France. One of the big wagons can be seen in the center of the group. The picture was taken just before it pulled out for its journey.

The picture at the bottom is a good sample of the dog and pony carts in which the small farmers of that district bring their poultry and eggs to market. In this country dogs are looked upon as rather expensive property, mostly because here the dogs are kept more for sport than work. In Belgium and Holland, dogs perform many kinds of work throughout the day—transporting good sized loads of garden truck from the fields. The big churning wheels are also worked by the dogs and when it comes to market day three dogs pull a cart that would make a load for a good sized pony. They faithfully watch the cart in the market place. We saw hundreds of these dogs hitched to carts in the markets of cities in Belgium and Holland and never saw one unruly or that tried to leave his post. However, I imagine that they are not honored to work in the market team until so well trained that they can be thoroughly trusted.

Mr. Vander Snickt's description of the Campine egg is worthy of considerable study. He said: "It must be round at both ends. The yolk is one-fourth larger in the egg that is round at both ends, than when one end is elongated or pointed.

"The egg should be white with matted surface—not shining.

"The shell must be resistant and strong.

"An important quality of the egg is the skin under the shell—it should be so resistant that if the shell becomes cracked the white cannot run out.

"The white of the egg must be very glutinous and keep well together around the yolk for making poached eggs.

"Enveloping the yolk also is a thin skin. This must be strong to contain the yolk when subjected to rough handling when shipped.

"The yolk must be rich in orange color and good flavor.

"Good taste results when the hens are running on humid pastures where there are many insects and rich, tender grasses—although when the hens are eating many beetles the eggs are of bad flavor. The best flavor comes to eggs when hens run on low pasture land.

"Iron, insects, and green food give color to the yolk.

"In small eggs, the eggs are much cheaper in proportion than the size warrants.

The two extra grammes of the large eggs of Audenarde, bring a much larger proportionate price than eggs in other Belgian markets when eggs are not quite so large are offered in competition with them."

We saw in England grade—14, 16, 20 and 24 eggs for a shilling. In this the lesson of the large egg is forcefully taught.

Campines for Pleasure and Profit

Some Thoughts on the Advantages of Poultry Rearing Over the Professions and Other Business—The Author Now Devotes His Entire Time to Campines—Took Up Campines First and After Comparing Them Side by Side With Other Breeds Prefers Them

By Dr. J. H. Prudhomme, Thurmont, Maryland

JUST a word about myself. I wish to say that I gave up my business in Baltimore City, Maryland, to come out here to Thurmont, at the root of the beautiful Blue Ridge Mountains, high, dry and healthful, 60 miles from Baltimore, primarily to raise chickens and to get away from the din and clatter of the city with its surfeit of humans, to get out with nature, therefore, secondarily, for the benefit of us all, my children in particular, of whom we have four. There is nothing in God's great world so good as pure mountain air, rich in the life giving property of ozone, and also pure, crystal, sparkling waters. We have been here now, going on five years, the city with its glamour has no attractions for us. This is why we are here at Thurmont.

Now, about the chickens. Well, when I was in the city I got the chicken fever, had it in my bones. I longed for the country, "back to the land," "back to nature." I studied poultry culture about a year before, finally making up my mind to make a change. In the course of time we landed at Thurmont.

In studying the different breeds of chickens none appealed to me so much as the Campines. I thought they were a remarkably beautiful fowl, with characteristics all their own and different from most all other breeds. I

thought them unique; then too they are great layers; a medium sized fowl, with a splendid breast development, small eaters, great rangers—it was the Campine for mine from the start. But, I was not satisfied with all that was said in favor of Campines, so like all novices, I took on other breeds for experimental purposes and for comparison, so I have bred White and Barred Rocks, R. I. Reds, Black Minorcas, Houdans; had an experience with Anconas, bred White Leghorns and also the White, Fawn and White, and Penciled Runner Ducks. Truly, I must say, after these years with the different breeds side by side, I am still partial to my first love—Campines for mine for ever more.

Now, kind reader, why is it, do you think, I took up poultry culture? Quite a descent from professional work, I suppose in your mind you must say: I don't find it so. I place poultry raising on par with the professions. You know poultry rearing in its different branches is today one of the great businesses of the country, amounting to nearly one billion dollars. Space forbids, or I would like to tell you of the opportunities and the advantages poultry offers over the professions, such as medicine, dentistry, the law, over manufacturing, merchandising, general farming, over stock raising and dairying, the keeping of cows for milk. You know in the poultry business you have the whole world to draw from. If you have something good to offer the world will make a beaten path to your door.

Just a brief comparison. Take the professions enumerated above. It requires seven years to go through school and four years to acquire a degree, eleven years. Then what? You either annex yourself to some hospital in order to become more proficient or join forces with some other practitioner, or you strike out alone and rent a small office, furnish it and wait for business to come. You can in your own mind draw the picture of the young doctor, or dentist or lawyer just out, sitting and waiting in his office for business to come. Thousands see the sign, the "shingle" as it is called, but pass on by; occasionally one drops in, and so it takes years to build up, to acquire fame, to attain success. And then, even in a large city, the circle is limited, you can't treat a patient in Canada, nor in South America, nor can you argue a law case in Mexico, but you can advertise, do an international business, sell eggs or live poultry any-

where, in Canada, South America, Mexico, etc. You have the whole world to draw from. Then, too, one can build up, start small and grow big, in remarkably less time than a professional man.

How many of us have the money to establish a manufacturing plant? It requires large capital. When established it requires more money along with brains to meet competition, introduce the new line to the trade, to the jobber, the wholesaler and the retailer. All these take a slice out of the original profit. It requires high salaried, expert salesmen along with traveling expenses, to introduce the goods.

General farming. It is not every one who has the health, the strength, the brawn, the muscular power sufficient to take hold of the plow handle, to harrow, to cultivate and to harvest the crop. This spells work—I believe farmers are born and not made. Of all the businesses the farmer's lot is a serious one, with a sequence of either too much rain to damage the crops, or no rain at all, with severe drought and the growing produce parches up; or there is the 17 year locust after the

CHAMPION SILVER CAMPINE COCKEREL FIRST AT N.Y.FAIR,N.Y.CITY,ALLENTOWN,HAGERSTOWN AND FREDERICK,1913 SILVER CAMPINE PULLET,FIRST AT N.Y.FAIR N.Y.CITY AND AT FREDERICK,MD,1913   BOTH OWNED AND SHOWN BY DR.J.H.PRUDHOMME,THURMONT,MARYLAND.

Fanciers throughout the country are showing much pleasure over the interesting color pattern of plumage that these Belgian beauties present, and no one can help admiring their sturdy, plump forms. There are plenty of problems in breeding them to Standard ideals that fascinate the fancier, and their big white eggs say volumes to those who cater to the highest paying markets, of their value during the seasons when their eggs do not trade even for dollars for the purpose of hatching show fowls. It takes but a glance at the above models to see that Dr. Prudhomme has gone in for the best, and the more you study them the more you are impressed that there is a good future for the Campines and that their success in America depends only on the way in which breeders place them before the public.—F. L. Sewell.

wheat, or the boll weavil devastating the cotton, or the corn won't, in bad season, germinate, or the potatoes get the blight, and what not. It is work, work, work all the time, and in the end there is very little surplus left over.

Now, you may say stock raising is a fine business, nearly every one likes animals. It requires a large farm, which costs money to buy, large expensive buildings, barns and the like, and also expensive blooded animals with which to make a start. It is a heavy line of work, too. But there is one thing in that line that does not appeal to me, and that is shipping. When you ship a horse, or a cow, or a sheep, or a swine, considerable trouble is attached to it. One has to see about engaging a box car, or if smaller animals, a heavy crate has to be made, etc. Now, with poultry, eggs are easily packed and shipped, and live birds are placed in light carriers, which can be easily taken in the gasoline buggy and carried to the express office.

Dairying or the milk business. An extensive business, nearly every one drinks milk. Like stock raising, same requires considerable money to start with, farm, barns, out buildings, etc., and who is it that wants to crawl out at 4 A. M., when the mercury in the bulb is flirting around zero, to milk a cow for some city sport? With poultry one can use an automatic feeder and sleep till the sun gets up.

Then merchandising. That is a splendid business you say. Well, it would be if it could be run on a cash, pay in advance basis, but so large a per cent is lost in crediting there is not much in being a merchant. It too, also requires considerable capital to stock up with. Lately I had an experience with a Brooklyn grocery which I offer as concrete proof to substantiate my argument. As I said I was shipping eggs, Leghorn eggs, to a large grocery in Brooklyn. They claimed to buy direct from the producer and sold to the consumer. I was getting a premium over New York market highest quotations, with no commission to pay. I received a letter from the merchandiser that he could not collect

from customers who owed him, that they would not pay and he was compelled to have a receiver appointed. He said he would pay me for last shipment as soon as he could, with 5 per cent interest, etc. So much for merchandising.

Now, in the fancy poultry business, everything is in advance, pay in advance, one gets the money, it is a sure thing. I would like to see more engage in the fancy poultry business. I do not know of a breed that offers better opportunities than Campines—Silvers or Goldens. Campines are a comparatively new breed over here, as most every one knows, and that they are an old breed in the old country, having been bred for hundreds of years over there in Belgium for eggs. They are a strikingly handsome fowl, there are none other just like them, they are rightly a dual purpose fowl; unique, pretty to look at on the lawn, and useful to fill the egg basket; that is what most everyone wants in a chicken anyway.

In the Campine one gets both, beauty and utility. Then, one's neighbor has not the same breed, another advantage. You can tell your chickens from all the chickens in your community, which alone is a great point. If they are stolen, if you can trace that peculiarly barred feather on someone else's property, you have evidence sufficient to call in a Burns detective, or the dictograph.

For the suburbanite the Campine is just the thing. Beautiful, clean, trim, spic and span, handsome in its business suit of a black feather with green, glossy sheen checked with delicate white stripe; they would make anyone's neighbors sit up and take notice. For the egg farmer or poultryman who probably does not care what a chicken looks like, but who want eggs, the Campine is just the thing, for they lay and they pay. They are little eaters and will forage more and hustle greater for subsistance in sunshine or storm, or will remain out in the wind or rain longer in proportion than any other fowl of which I know.

The Campines as Money Makers

The Interest in Campines is Great and Wide Spread—Their Present Popularity is Due Chiefly to Their Egg-Laying Ability— What a Flock of Campines, Averaging 300 Birds, Consumed During Nine Months, How They Were Cared for and the Number and Value of the Eggs— What 1,600 Campines, Properly Housed and Fed, are Expected to Do—Campines as Market Fowl—Small Eaters—Heavy Layers

By J. Fred N. Kennedy, Birch Cliff, Ont., Canada

THE interest that has been taken in the Campine fowl during the past three years is really amazing. In about three years' time I have received nearly 20,000 letters, all inquiring into the merits and future of this truly wonderful little fowl, so whenever I am able to present new facts pertaining to them it affords me the greatest of pleasure.

Beginning the first day of January, 1913, I set aside 325 Campine females, both Golden and Silver, to make up my breeding pens for the coming season. A little over 100 of them were from one to five years old—yes, some were even older. About 225 were pullets or 1912-bred birds, and of these 225 birds, two-thirds were birds that were bred and raised in England by my partner,

the Rev. E. Lewis Jones. Nearly all the older birds were imported stock, and they had gone through the severe winter of 1911-1912, when the temperature registered as low as 32 degrees below zero. All these birds were kept in open-front houses of my own design.

I shall find pleasure in giving some idea of the manner in which I have handled my birds and the results obtained commercially, from the first of January through the winter, spring and summer up to the first of October, being nine months, or 273 days. During that time I sold a few of the females for breeding purposes, also had a few die, which left me with 276 at the end of the nine months, so I had on an average, say, 300 birds during the entire time.

These 300 birds consumed about 5,808 pounds of dry mash, which is kept before them all the time in hoppers, and which was compounded and cost as follows:

Oat flour, 1,532 lbs., cost $26.04
Wheat shorts, 1,532 lbs., cost 19.15
Bran, 1,532 lbs., cost 17.62
Beef scrap or meal, 553 lbs., cost 14.94
Bone meal, 252 lbs., cost 5.70
Alfalfa meal, 250 lbs., cost 5.25
Charcoal, 100 lbs., cost 1.20
Salt, 57 lbs., cost .... .57
                                                                        ———
Total, 5,808 lbs., cost.................................$90.47

My birds also consumed about 600 pounds of oyster shell and grit, which cost $3.60. I kept it in a small hopper directly above the dry mash hopper, so that whatever they wasted fell into the dry mash below. I used straw for litter and used in the nine months about 5,205 pounds, costing $37.85. I wish to mention that I purchased my straw baled and noticed quite often on opening the bales that the straw had a tendency to be musty, which is certainly very bad for the fowls and should be avoided. I propose this coming season to use peat moss, as used by Mr. Jones, and I believe the results will be much better. For every fifteen birds I scattered in the litter every morning a heaped half pint of mixed grain; about one hour before sunset they had a heaped pint of the same. They were fed in all about 6,751 pounds of grain, compounded and costing as follows:

Wheat, 3,375 lbs., cost ....$ 56.25
Cracked corn, 1,688 lbs., cost 25.32
Oats, 1,688 lbs., cost 19.86
                                                                        ———
Total, 6,751 lbs., cost $101.43

At 11:30 A. M. every day the 300 birds got all the green food they would eat up clean in about fifteen minutes. At the first part of the season I used a ton of giant sugar beets, costing $6.00. After using them up I went back to my old plan of sprouting oats, and really found them much more satisfactory, especially for breeders. I used in all 1,088 pounds of oats for sprouting, costing $12.80.

Now, to sum up the total amount of food consumed by my 300 Campine females during the nine months and the cost of same, I find it is as follows:
5,809 lbs. dry mash, cost ....$ 90.47
6,751 lbs. mixed grain, cost 101.43
600 lbs. oyster shell and grit, cost 3.60
5,205 lbs. straw for litter, cost 37.85
1,088 lbs. oats for sprouting, cost 12.80
2,000 lbs. giant sugar beets, cost 6.00
                                                                        ———
Total cost $252.15

The Egg Yield

The returns received during the nine months from the 300 Campine females were 38,651 eggs. Of course, only a few of the eggs were marketed, as during the breeding season nearly all were used for incubation on the farm or sold for hatching purposes, but in making

FIRST PRIZE COCKEREL AND HEN
WINNERS AT MADISON SQUARE GARDEN, DEC. 1911, OWNED BY J. FRED N. KENNEDY
BIRCH CLIFF, ONTARIO, CANADA.

Among the old established races of continental Europe whose charming plumage and elegant form have been improved during recent years by fanciers of Great Britain, none is more fascinating to the eye—and perhaps more profitable on account of its large, white eggs—than the Campine, originally of Belgium. Rev. E. Lewis Jones, Radnorshire, England, the foremost British promoter of the breed, visited Madison Square Garden with some of his choicest specimens, Dec., 1911, and the above pair, cockerel and hen, won first and were purchased by J. Fred N. Kennedy.—F. L. Sewell.

up my calculations for this article, we will suppose that the 38,651 eggs were all sold to supply the ready market. In Toronto, Canada, near which my farm is situated, during the past season restaurants and hotels were only too willing to make contracts for strictly new laid eggs at the rate of 36 cents a dozen, or 3 cents each, which makes the market value of my 38,651 eggs $1,159.53. I have already shown that the total cost of maintaining the 300 birds was $252.15, which leaves a profit of $907.38, or a little over $3.00 on each bird for nine months. I assure you, kind reader, I am certainly very proud of these facts and figures, under the conditions.

I suppose, in the mind of the general public, this egg yield is nothing extraord'nary, but I think it is when one considers that over two-thirds of the birds were imported and one-third of them was from two to five years old, saying nothing of the fact that the birds had not been bred scientifically for egg production.

I do not think anyone has kept a trap-nest record of Campines for any length of time, following up the results solely for the production of a heavy laying strain. My partner, the Rev. Jones, in England, and I here, have had our hands full up to date trying to produce birds enough to meet the demand of our many customers all over the world, so when I take into consideration these conditions, I regard the results as very gratifying, indeed, and much better than I anticipated.

Small Eaters—Heavy Layers

No one will deny that a profit of a little over $900.00 on 300 birds, or $3.00 a bird for nine months, was very satisfactory, and yet the egg yield was nothing out of the ordinary. The surprise lies in the small amount of food consumed. It costs only 84.05 cents to maintain a Campine female for nine months, or a little over 9 cents a month. The secret of the Campine's success as an egg machine is the small amount of food consumed for the large number of eggs produced. I do not consider my system of feeding perfect, and I certainly hope to improve on it the coming season, but during the past season I have managed to feed my birds at a less cost and obtained greater results than I have done heretofore.

Another thing that helps Campines to attain big results is that they are non-sitters and they spread their egg laying all the year round, not being sprinters at certain seasons. As the season advanced I suppose I had ten or fifteen birds that showed signs of broodiness. Some would be on the nest during the day, but at night you would find them back on the roost. A few that would stick were set, but nearly every other one would give up before the 21 days were gone and wanted to go back to real business again.

During my years of experience with poultry I have kept nearly every noted variety, in fact, the past season I had four pens of other varieties for the sole purpose of watching and comparing results, and I must say for the little Campines, although they have not as yet been scientifically bred for egg production, that they do, in a flock, out-class all other breeds it has been my pleasure to experiment with, when it comes to laying large white eggs and lots of them for the small amount of food consumed. Mr. F. L. Platt, when he called the Campine hen "a heavy layer of heavy eggs," told the poultry public in six words what the Campine really is, but I would add, "at small cost," calling them "heavy layers of heavy eggs at small cost."

The coming season I am going to devote a lot of time and study to my matings along the lines of scientific breeding for a heavy egg production. Campines must stand or fall by their qualities as egg layers, and with the foundation we already have to work upon, success is sure.

Campines As Market Fowl

I hear a criticizing reader say, "The laying results are all very well, but how about marketing your surplus cockerels?"

In answer to this I wish to say, the true test of the table value of any bird is the percentage of meat that it will yield and not its mere weight. The ideal table bird then must be small and fine in bone and must be trimly built with a frame suitable for carrying a lot of breast meat. A pheasant will yield nearly three-quarters as much meat as the ordinary fowl which has double its weight. The excellence of the Campine as a table fowl lies in the fact that it yields as high a percentage as any other variety, and in many cases much more. The young stock matures very quickly, especially the cockerels, and this enables the commercial plant to market them early, as they are plump as partridges, especially when the chicks are from eight to ten weeks old. Again, the pullets mature just as quickly in proportion, and begin to lay, if properly raised and cared for, at eighteen to twenty-two weeks old. I had this season over 150 pullets begin laying at the age of eighteen and twenty weeks.

Some will say that they do not like pullets that begin to lay too early; neither do I, if it is not their nature, but it is the Campine's nature to mature early, and it is natural for the little Campine pullet to begin to lay at a very early age. Of course, there are exceptional cases, just the same as you will find in every other variety. You no doubt have read of Rocks and Wyandottes laying at twenty weeks old. This is too early, because it is not natural for them, and such precocious birds can never develop the size characteristic of the big boned races. I have had several customers report to me that they had Campine pullets laying at less than fifteen weeks old. I have heard of them beginning to lay at thirteen and one-half weeks, and I have no reason to doubt the claim, but it is not natural, just as it is not natural for a Rock to lay at twenty weeks.

I hope my readers understand what I am trying to explain and that they will not condemn the Campine pullets for laying so young and think it deteriorates their breeding qualities, because it is really natural for them to do so. Besides, everyone will admit that every egg means money. When you take into consideration that they begin to lay from six to eight weeks earlier than the American and English varieties, laying, say, 30 to 40 eggs before the latter begins to lay and that they cost easily one-third less to keep, can you realize the difference in profit? Did you ever think of it in that way before?

I am now planning to build another house of my own design to take care of 1,600 layers and I expect to have it in readiness for next season. I shall fill it with Campines as fast as I can, for I know what they can and will do for me, because my past experience with them has taught me. I estimate that 1,600 Campine females properly housed and properly fed, with a little help along the line of being bred-to-lay, should yield me in eggs, properly marketed, after paying all cost of feeds, etc., fully $5,000.00 a year.

The Housing and Care of Campines

The Stock Should Not be Overfed—Range Desirable for the Young Birds--A Fine Type of House for Campine Breeders Described—The Materials Cost $11—The Campine as a Utility Fowl

By Gensemer Bros., Creston, Ohio

THE Campines are, we believe, superior to any other of the non-setting breeds. They will produce more eggs on the minimum amount of food and if given their freedom are practically self sustaining. They will forage over a wide territory, always keeping in good condition and laying a surprisingly large number of eggs. People who are unacquainted with the breed are inclined to over feed, as it is hard for them to realize that they can exist and lay on so small an amount. They have been bred for centuries in a dry, barren country where practically nothing grew, where they were compelled to forage for their living. The climate of their native country (La Campine, Belgium) is variable, alternating from extreme heat to severe cold. These climatic conditions have contributed to their hardiness so that they will flourish under the most adverse circumstances. We believe that they will stand more hard usage and neglect than any other breed, but on the other hand, they appreciate good care and kind treatment and will show their appreciation in a substantial manner. They will also evince a genuine affection for the one who cares for them.

They stand confinement equally as well or better than other and larger breeds. One strong point in their favor is that they are always clean and neat looking. A large flock of either color makes a very pretty sight, with their beautiful markings, together with bright red single combs, nearly black eye, and clean, neat, leaden-blue legs. They are very attractive.

A great many of our customers inquire as to the merits of the two colors. We find them to be equal in hardiness, egg production and precocity. There has been an idea extant that Campines were hard to raise, being constitutionally weak. We will admit that there have been grounds for this belief in the past, but since becoming acclimated we find them just as hardy and as easily raised as the chicks of any other breed. We have found that to be successful in the rearing of the chicks of any breed it is necessary to have suitable coops, sufficiently large so that the chicks can be confined comfortably during wet weather, and until the grass is dry every morning, also that chicks and coop should be kept free from vermin, that chicks should be fed good sweet grain, with a sufficient amount of clean water and an ample supply of milk, either sweet or sour.

The young birds after feathering nicely do remarkably well if placed on range in colony houses, with a supply of good mash in self feeders, to which they can have constant access and a light feed of grain (preferably wheat) in the evening, of which they consume a very small amount. Their crops are usually filled to capacity, as there are but very few insects that escape

them and the exercise they receive in securing same develops them properly and symmetrically.

We find that it accrues to the advantage of the birds to be allowed to roost in the trees until freezing weather. We made no attempt last fall to house our young stock until the first heavy fall of snow and never before started the winter with as healthy a lot of birds. With the exception of a few slight colds, we have not had a sick bird this season.

Our four years' experience with this breed leads us to believe that they are the ideal fowl for large egg farms that specialize on eggs for market. Their eggs being of large size and pure white will naturally appeal to the consumer; the fact that they do well in confinement, in large flocks, and will produce eggs at a time

HOUSES AND RANGE ON PLANT OF GENSEMER BROS.

when they are worth the most money, should commend them to the market poultryman.

As a table fowl they are especially fine, as they produce an abundance of breast meat. The ideal table bird must be small and fine in bone and must be trimly built, with a form suitable for carrying a lot of breast meat. Campine chicks eight to ten weeks old are as plump as partridges and are remarkably good eating. The Roman Epicures in Julius Ceasar's time pronounced their flesh "Food for the Gods."

Good House for Campines

Proper housing contributes largely to the successful handling of Campines. They, like all large combed breeds, should be kept during zero weather in practically frost proof houses. We experimented with houses several years endeavoring to construct one that would supply an ample amount of fresh air as well as protect their combs from frost. We have at last, we believe, solved the problem. We gave the house a pretty severe test this last winter, especially during one month of zero weather with thermometer 24 below several mornings without a frosted comb, but birds in large houses and barn had combs badly frosted. We feel justified in recommending this house to Campine breeders.

This is a house in which the birds will be comfortable the entire year, there being but very little space for the birds to heat in cold weather. If filled to capacity they will remain comfortable through the coldest night.

By feeding their grain in deep litter in the scratching compartment, they will be afforded sufficient exercise. We place the house on blocks about twelve inches high and in hot weather during the heat of the day the birds will be found under the house, where it is always cool.

The house is twelve feet long, four feet wide, three feet high in the rear and four feet in front, having a division in center with small door for birds to pass from one compartment to the other; the right half of house being designed for roosting and laying compartment, the other half for scratching room; the roost six feet long, extends across the back of roosting room with dropping board beneath. The water fountain is placed on raised platform at right of door in the corner; the self-feeders and nests are placed within reach of the door, making it unnecessary for the attendant to enter the house. We have screens over all openings, but we use window in opening in roosting room during the cold months, but have an opening in the door about 18x24 covered by muslin, also muslin curtains for scratching room openings. The house is constructed in such a manner as to be air tight except the front openings.

This house will accommodate ten adult Campines. It can be easily moved and is fine to house young stock on range.

In constructing house we use white pine for siding, hard pine for partitions, flooring and roof, finally covering roof with some good roofing material, bringing it down and fastening under the eaves with slats, thus rendering it air tight. The material for this house costs about $11.00.

The Treatment of Sick Birds

Imported Stock Not Being Fitted to It's New Environment Not Only Requires Good Care, But Should the Birds Get Out of Condition Quick Remedies are Necessary — Peat Moss Recommended as a Substitute for Straw—If a Very Sick Bird Does Not Respond to Treatment, it is Best to Kill Him and Thus Eliminate Him From the Flock—Valuable Formulas

By Jos. F. Chapman, Brackenridge, Pa.

CAMPINES two or three years ago were looked upon as a "boom" breed. Fanciers, practical poultrymen and people who just kept chickens, were to be convinced. The Campine hen, however, has shown that she is a business bird and when it comes down to looks it must be conceded that she is "some chicken." Campines have demonstrated their wonderful utility, and as an artistic creation cannot be surpassed.

As everyone knows, it is the English to whom we are indebted for the improved Campine. Consequently all of our foundation stock has been imported and there are still large numbers of birds coming over. We therefore must recognize the fact that these have been subjected to a complete change of climate and in many cases of housing. It is therefore natural to expect this stock to be a little more susceptible than domestic grown birds. And it is in regard to this rather than a discussion of the breed that I speak of.

To my mind there are three avoidable causes for these troubles, improper housing, feeding and litter. In housing I advocate smaller coops or if large, deep coops are used partitions should be well extended not less than six feet, to break up all possible drafts. In severe weather a curtain is all right, but it certainly should be arranged to give plenty of ventilation. Bringing a bird down out of a warm moist roost to a very cold coop will start a cold.

One of the really difficult things in handling Campines is to feed them little enough. An over-fed bird is sure to give trouble in time. I think, however, that straw litter has had more to do with troubles in these birds than any other one cause. Remember that your birds are working in material entirely different to that they were raised on and that in the dust arising there are countless fungus (mildew) and microbes they never breathed before. Since adapting peat moss and deep roosting closets my troubles have ceased.

In the treatment of simple colds and throat irritations I found the following fairly effective:

Menthol, 30 grains; camphor, 30 grains; thymol, 15 grains; crude oil, one pint.

Put in a pint bottle, warm slightly till liquified and add the crude oil. This is injected in the nostrils and cleft and also used for swabbing the throat. Where there are a few sniffy colds in the flock, pour a little on the drinking water. When an infected bird is found all drinking vessels should be mopped out with crude carbolic acid and then scalded. If a case does not respond to treatment in a reasonable time, unless the bird is a valuable one, it does not pay to put the needed time in doctoring nor to run the risk of infecting the rest of your flock.

If the throat is severely affected there are several treatments: 1 oz. spirits of turpentine and 30 drops Tr. capsicum applied a few times only. A ten per cent sol. nitrate of silver applied lightly to top of the wind pipe will prevent choking. All birds should be given heavy doses of epsom salts, one-half to one teaspoonful. Other throat treatment consists of applying sulphur or powdered chlorate of potash. A good treatment also will be found in tincture iron and glycerine, each one-half ounce, and 30 grains chlor. potash. Apply to spots or swab throat lightly. If treating several cases at the same time do not use the same swab on all, as your troubles will only grow if it is a contagious disease.

For coughs and colds 3 ounces syrup white pine and one dram iodine of potash, giving 10 to 30 drops every 3 or 4 hours. A good many of these cases are accompanied by wheezing, for which tincture benzoin compound one tablespoonful is added to one pint of boiling water, allowing the bird to inhale steam. Equal parts of carbolic acid and tincture iodine may be used in the same way or dropped on something hot enough to vaporize it. A splendid all around salve consists of sulphur ointment, to which has been added 5 per cent of creolin.

Where birds have had serious troubles there is only one way to disinfect a coop. Clean out and spray with carbolic and crude oil. Then get two granite dishes. In one burn one-fourth pound of sulphur, using something to keep it away from the floor. In the other one pour one pint of solution formaldehyde. Place this over an alcohol stove (operated very cheaply with wood alcohol) so that it will boil. Close down your curtains and leave

coop closed for four hours at least. Open up and air three or four hours before replacing stock. This refers to coop 12x16.

To those who are interested in well-bred stock and not conversant with its treatment, I would suggest they secure a copy of Reliable Poultry Remedies, issued by R. P. J., and at intervals spend a half hour or so acquainting themselves with the most prevalent diseases of poultry. It may save you some very distressing experiences—which others have had.

The Campine Fowl

The Utility Qualities of English and Continental Breeds are Attracting the Attention of American Breeders —Early History of One Strain of the Golden Campines—One Distinction of the Campine is Their Extreme Tameness — While Early Eggs Do Not Run Fertile the Late Hatched Birds Make Up by Fast Growing

By Aug. D. Arnold, Dillsburg, Pa.

THOSE who have bred the Campine fowl for a few years cannot help but be in love with it and the question will naturally come to such persons why it is that the Campine with all its good qualities has been bred for hundreds of years and yet never was taken up by English and American breeders until only a few years ago. The chief reason may possibly be that fanciers have not recognized the utility qualities and only the fancy part of the Campine was considered, and it was only after the plumage of the Campine was pleasing to the fancier of England and America that this breed was taken in hand by them, and we may say right here that while the fancy part of the great poultry industry has many adherents, it is a fact that the utility side is on the move as it never has been before. Americans are getting into this country the best utility fowls to be found in England, France and Belgium, and a very marked interest is taking hold of poultrymen of America, and the American Poultry Association is taking notice of this fact and acting accordingly.

While the Campine is also a good table fowl, the chief quality claimed for them is their great laying qualities, laying a white egg of good size and plenty of them, and their beauty as a show bird is being admired more and more as they improve in plumage as they do from year to year. This they are doing at a very rapid pace and especially is this true of the Goldens. It is not over three years ago that the first Goldens were put on exhibition at the Palace Show in England and Madison Square, New York. Since their first appearance in the show room they have had many admirers and the improvement in this variety has been simply wonderful.

While the Silvers have been bred for hen-feathered males for ten or twelve years, and the Goldens for only two or three years, yet it is a fact that the Goldens are ahead of them in all fancy points and lead them in hardiness, and as utility fowls they are in every way the equal of the Silvers.

There is a bit of history connected with the introduction of the Golden Campine into this country that is not known even by our leading breeders of Campines. The Golden Campine was brought into this country at least two or three years before the Rev. Mr. Jones exhibited them while on his visit to America. We refer

to his exhibit at Madison Square Garden, December, 1911.

The first Golden Campines were brought to this country by Mr. White of Frederick, Md. Mr. White being a dealer of Belgian horses, made a number of trips to Belgium and while attending a horse show in Belgium on one of these visits, he was presented with a pen of Golden Campines by the King of Belgium. Mr. White bred these birds for a few years, giving stock and eggs to his neighbors, as they proved to be very great layers of large white eggs. He also gave a setting of these eggs to a Mr. Hawkins of Pennsylvania. While we were looking over Mr. Jones' pen of Goldens at Madison Square Garden, Mr. Theo. Wittman of Allentown, Pa., came up to the coop, and after looking at them, he told us that he knew a man in the country in which we lived who had Golden Campines for several years, stating that he had seen them (these being the birds Mr. Hawkins owned). We thought at the time that Mr. Wittman was surely mistaken, but on our return from the New York Show we at once wrote Mr. Hawkins, and in answer he wrote that he had received a setting of eggs from Mr. White of Frederick, Md., and raised the fowls, and stated since he had no male, he would sell the birds to me. I at once ordered them. Mr. Hawkins wrote me they were wonderful layers. Through Mr. Hawkins I got the address of Mr. White and bought twenty-five females, then we imported a male from an English breeder, also had Mr. Kennedy, of Birch Cliff, Ont., Canada, order one pen from the Rev. Mr. Jones for us.

This cross has given us a strain no other breeder owns, giving vigor and stamina that could not be procured in any other way. Mr. White did not know that these birds were Campines until sometime after we bought them from him. While these birds were not bred from clear Braekel males, yet the females came in good markings and at least three of the leading breeders of Golden Campines in America have females in their yards that came from our flock, so it will be seen that the Golden Campine reached America before they were shown at any show in England.

One of the most notable characteristics of the Campine that is so different from all small varieties of fowls, is their extreme tameness. They are real pets. Another point in their favor is the very small amount of feed they consume, and when left on free range, they will hunt their own food. We believe the South is an ideal country for the Campine and if allowed on free range and left to roost in open shed they would do good work for their owners. Our birds are raised on farms and we find the Campines as they come in from this farm about November 10th to 15th are in the finest possible condition.

While the Campine stands confinement well, yet it is an active bird and free range suits it better, and under that condition it will do the most for its owner. One trouble we find with the Campine is they do not lay well fertilized eggs as a rule before the latter part of April or the first part of May. But we find Campines hatched in June and July mature in plenty of time for early spring hatching. Chicks when started grow exceedingly fast.

In conclusion we will say all who take up Campines will no doubt be pleased with them. The Rev. Mr. Jones says: "Once a Campinist always a Campinist." Now since the plumage is so much improved they are becoming a fancier's fowl that is beautiful to behold and in a few more years of improvement they will be one of our leading exhibition birds, as well as one of the greatest layers to be found.

The Silver Campine

This Article is Based on the Experience of One of Americas Leading Campine Breeders—As Layers, Campines Compare Favorably With Leghorns—The Third Generation of American Bred Campines Are Very Hardy—Correct Type and Color Discussed

By Frank E. Hering, South Bend, Ind.

SUFFICIENT has already been written concerning the history of the Campine and its ancient lineage through the Romans and Franks, who have preserved its fame in their chronicles. At the present time, it seems to me, those interested in this breed are concerned chiefly with two considerations. The first ot these is the present utility or commercial value of the breed, and the value it is likely to have in the future. Upon this point depends the wide-spread breeding and popularity of the Campine. Of secondary importance is the consideration of the physical characteristics that breeders should try to evolve.

Silver King II, a Silver Campine cockerel owned by Frank E. Hering, winner of 1st prize at the Coliseum Show, Chicago, December 12-17, 1913. Pronounced by competent judges to be the best cockerel of the year.

From my point of view the discussions of this breed that I have read, have too much theory and too little of actual observation. The opinions that I am expressing here are from personal experience and study of the Silver Campine. I do not desire my judgment to be taken as final.

On my plant, The Willows Farm, I have S. C. White Leghorns and Silver Campines. Thus I have had an opportunity to compare the relative merits of the two varieties. The Leghorns, of which I have about a thousand, are carefully bred and have won distinction in the leading show rooms of the country. My study has led me to several conclusions favorable to the Campine. I consider it as good a forager as the Leghorn and not nearly so shy. As a table bird, I should rank it higher, its meat being a bit more tender, and not so stringy. On an average, the Campine eggs are larger than the Leghorn eggs. At the present time I have a number of Campines, both hens and pullets, whose eggs are as large as those of any chicken eggs I have ever seen.

Whether or not the Campine lays as many eggs as the Leghorn I cannot yet say. My Leghorns are an exceptionally good laying strain and I do not think a few years' experience would justify me in drawing conclusions relative to the laying qualities of the Campine. During April the laying average of my Campines was between 55 and 60 per cent, and at the time of writing, May, the percentage remains about the same. I think that the number of eggs will depend very largely upon the strain. A Campine flock that has been carefully bred will lay just as well as a good egg-laying strain of Leghorns.

The hardiness of a breed is an important factor in determining its commercial value. I have found that the Campines stand extremes of heat and cold unusually well, but that they are susceptible to the poultry diseases occasioned by draughty houses and dampness. This is to be expected since the Campines are a recent importation into the country. The more severe climate of their new environment as compared with the climate of their original home in western Europe, is bound to make itself felt unless a fair measure of protection is given them. I am now raising my third generation of

Campines. Most of my chicks have been hatched in incubators and have been placed in Cornell brooder houses. Concerning my young stock that is now about three months old, the manager of my plant, Mr. Hiram Bradshaw, reports that never in his experience has there been so small mortality among his baby chicks. I do not believe that we have lost five per cent of the Campines hatched this spring.

I ascribe the manifest sturdiness of the third generation to two causes. The first cause is good parentage. All of my young stock are descended either through their male or female parent from Silver King 1, who, in addition to his other splendid physical points, was as healthy a specimen of Campine as I have ever seen. The second cause, I consider the hygienic surroundings provided for the chickens. My breeding houses are free from dampness at all times of the year. All of them have about one-third of the frontage open, and even in the coldest weather this third is covered only with muslin screens. The health of my young stock, I attribute largely to these two factors, dryness and fresh air.

It must be remembered, of course, that the physical condition of little chickens is dependent to a great extent upon their daily care. Mine, when permitted to exercise outside the brooder house have been placed in yards with a soil of light loam and in which there is little, if any, high vegetation. I learned last spring that heavy dew in the morning and long wet grass are fatal to the Campine chick.

To sum up my opinions as to the utility of the Campine stock, I believe that its hardiness, under fairly favorable conditions, will recommend it for breeding purposes; I feel confident that in the hands of any careful breeder, the Campine, in a very short time, will equal the egg production of the very best laying strains of Leghorns. Indeed, in my opinion, these two stocks will resemble one another more than any other of the lighter breeds.

As to the physical characteristics that add to the beauty and therefore the popularity of the fowl, I wish to see the Campine a sprightly creature, in type resembling the Leghorn much more than the Minorca. I would have the breast, especially in the females, a bit fuller than the breast of the Leghorn. In preference to the pronounced curve sought after in the back of the Leghorn, I would have the Campine's back slope a bit from the shoulders. In size and weight I think the Campine should fall a little more than the other breed. Beau Brummel, however, one of my Leghorn males, who has been a noted prize winner during the last four years, weighed seven pounds as a yearling! Now I should not like to see a Campine male, even a cock, considered as a standard toward which we should breed, whose weight exceeded six pounds.

At the present time, I favor allowing the breeder a wide latitude as to the feathering of Campines, with, perhaps, an agreement on such important considerations as color of hackle, width of white bar on the feather, and condition of the tail furnishings. It is very difficult to get a white hackle and well-barred wings and saddle in the same bird. If the feather-barring on the breast is strongly marked there is a tendency to in-

Claribel, First Prize Pullet Chicago Coliseum Show, December, 1913. Owned by Frank E. Hering.

determinate barring on the back. The establishment of all of these desirable characteristics can be obtained only by careful selection.

I believe that if we emphasize white hackles, as free as possible from ticking, wings with every feather barred, pronounced saddle hangers and tail furnishings with every feather barred to the end, we shall add greatly to the popularity of the breed. In the matter of barrings, I favor a ratio of between three and four to one between the white and the black bars, on all except the breast feathers. On these I think a ratio of one to one should be accepted for some time to come.

My strain has already contributed several valuable additions toward Campine perfection. Most important of these is the beautiful green sheen that I have been able to accentuate in the plumage of my young stock. Others are the regular and beautiful barrings of the sickle feathers, and the increase in length of sickles and saddle hangers. The first cockerel at the last show in the Coliseum, Chicago, had sickle feathers that measured fourteen inches in length and saddle hangers that measured between six and seven inches, at eight months of age. The tail of this bird and his brother—first pen cockerel—had an angle of about 45 degrees. Owing to the length of the tail feathers and the very heavy cushion across the saddle, the lines of these two males were as graceful as the lines of the Leghorn.

The Campine breed is new and the most of its varied possibilities are yet to be revealed. A few years spent in the study of it leaves much to be learned. For some time to come the interest of the breed will best be served by intelligent discussion and a free exchange of opinion among its friends.

Why We Are Breeding Golden Campines

The Foundation Was Laid by the Purchase of a Great Hen and the Importation of a Male—The Goldens Are the Best Variety by Test—The English Improved the Campines and it Now Rests With the American Breeder to Add the "Finishing Touches"—Americans Will Do Better to Buy at Home and Then Insist on Getting American Bred Birds

By A. A. Carver, Seville, Ohio

THE wonderful popularity of the Campine in England and Belgium, their spectacular entry into America, the beautiful cuts in the American journals, caused the writer to suggest to his wife that she take up the breeding of Campines in a small way. We talked the matter over at divers times. We would buy the best for our foundation and work for material rather than pecuniary results.

We would see how near perfection we could breed them and note their improvement year by year. Coming from a country of quiet, careful, painstaking people, into a hurley-burley country running mad with commercialism, these beauties would need real true friends who would place them above the dollar—friends who would give them homes and mate them in a small way, that their blood might flow out to beautify and make better their kin in the commercial world. With this thought paramount in our minds, the taking of a few of these beautiful birds and breeding them up to the highest possible standard, filled us with enthusiasm and brought into our hearts new hopes and pleasures that only come to the real true fancier.

Forthwith letters were fluttering hither and thither in quest of Golden Campines; England, Canada, the East. We were living the past over again. We learned of a great Golden Campine hen that was being exhibited at the Cleveland Show. She was reported as being the best seen on this side of the water. We were told by an old Barred Rock breeder who has been raising sensational Rocks for many years, that a great female mated to an inferior male brought better results than a superior male to an inferior female (and to breed the sensational we must mate the best to the best.) So this great Golden Campine hen became our property, and is now living amid her daughters and grand-daughters in the Campine hennery on Carver's Red Farms.

FIRST PRIZE GOLDEN CAMPINE COCK MADISON S. GARDEN, N.Y. DEC. 1913 BRED AND OWNED BY MANHATTAN FARMS   BRIGHTON, N.Y.

It is only a few years since it was a rare thing to find a hen feathered Golden Campine male, but today we see specimens at leading shows that approach the best Silvers in feather and markings. Madison Square Garden Show had an excellent class of Goldens in the season of 1913-14, and among them were some specimens that were truly wonders for clear barring of rich golden bay over a glossy black ground color. The cock shown above was winner of first prize. He was a remarkable specimen in color, having a splendid barred back and wing, also a well marked breast, with barring that extended well up on the throat, while his sickle feathers gave strong indications of barring their entire length.—A. O. Schilling.

The "Empress" we have named her, being the mother of our elect, the first pen pullets, Chicago.

We must have a male bird her equal, and as none could be found this side of the water, we imported direct from Rev. E. Lewis Jones, her mate, who has since won 1st in the pen at the Chicago Coliseum Show, and one of the best ever shown in America. This bird is now mated to Empress and her daughters.

It is now May 10th and we have cockerels and pullets almost large enough to exhibit; early spring hatched chicks, showing the wonderful growth and vitality of the Goldens when properly bred and mated. As regarding fast growers, heavy layers of large marketable eggs, beautiful plumage and type, we place the Goldens first of the Campines, and as soon as they become better known, we believe, they will rank with the Campines as White Leghorns do in Leghorndom.

We experimented with Silvers the first year, carefully comparing them with Goldens. Now Carver's Red Farms breed only the latter. To our poultry friends who are unacquainted with Campines, we say, compare them, for they are winners and will stand the test.

The Golden Campines have proven extraordinary layers with us of large uniform white eggs, with the exception of possibly three or four hens in our matings showing tinted eggs. By careful selection and restriction we will soon eliminate this from the Goldens. This is a feature, I think, the English and Belgian fanciers have neglected, and which the American fancier will quickly weed out. It seems that the Campine has improved as it migrated and it is up to the fanciers of this country to put the finishing touches to its beauty and usefulness, by breeding for better type and eggs, since its laying qualities will be hard to improve, as well as its beautiful plumage. The Golden Campines owe much to their noted English friend, Rev. E. Lewis

Jones, who has painted their feathers with a master hand and beautified them beyond description. The chances are that very few breeders in this country will ever realize what this great English preacher did for the Golden Campines. The results of this master artist in the mating of Golden Campines will be everlasting and far-reaching. He and we will be on the other side of the grave, but his good work will be left in the blood of these beautiful Campines that will grace the yards of the thousands to follow.

We believe the demand for Golden Campines will steadily grow as they become better known to the American fancier. They have had the disadvantage of following in the wake of the Silver Campine; hence have not been so much talked about and exhibited, but unless we are mightily mistaken the old saying of "Last, but not least," will be emphasized good and strong as soon as the American becomes educated.

The demand this year has been extraordinary, considering the newness of the breed, and the future looks very bright for those who will take them up and breed them in a careful, painstaking way. For the small select breeder the Golden Campines are adapted, for they meet the high ideals of the true fancier and lover of the beautiful, being of a more gentle disposition than the Silvers, not so inclined to the wild nature, and are easily handled and confined.

Our experience in showing Golden Campines is that they are bound to prove one of the most popular varieties in the show room. At the Chicago Show great crowds thronged the aisles to get a glimpse of the Campines, and outside of the Rhode Island Reds, they were the center of attraction, and we predict even greater interest at that show from year to year as they become better known.

Regarding our experience with imported birds, we can see a marked improvement in vitality in the second generation, showing the Campine to be a very hardy chicken when fully acclimated. There is a very marked improvement in our last year's hatch over the year previous, both in vigor and laying.

The last crop seems to have a more finished appearance and do not mind the weather so much. We believe it takes three or four generations to fully acclimate imported Campines.

We believe the American fancier will do well to buy at home rather than to import, since the early importers now have yards equal to the English and from now on there will be nothing gained by going abroad for their birds. We feel we now have birds of our own raising fit to hold their own in the show room with any imported birds that may be brought over. It is certain we can show a more rugged, healthy, vigorous bird, and those who now import will have to start where we started and be that much behind in vigor and vitality. We are now so sure of our footing that we would not pay the carriage on imported Golden Campines with the expectation of improving our yards. It is not our intention of breeding, or keeping rather, any large number of matings of Goldens on Carver's Red Farms, but rather to breed them in a small intensive way and see how good we can get them. As with our Rhode Island Reds we shall keep our ideals high and our matings trimmed close, that there may be pleasure as well as profit in the work.

Heyope Rectory,
Knighton, Radnorshire.

Dear Mr. Jacobus:—

It is pronounced KAM-PEEN.

The word CAMPINE is French and the method of pronouncing it is as above.

We in English are accustomed to the word pine for a kind of tree and at first 80 per cent of the people pronounced it as if it were KAM-PINE, but really the INE is pronounced as EEN in queen.

Yours faithfully,
E. LEWIS JONES.

"Get a Few"

By H. P. McDonough, Newark, New York

BY this time, with all the information given through the press, the majority of us know how and when the Campines came into prominence; ancient history does not concern the majority of breeders—"Efficiency" is the watch word of all good business, why not have a greater "efficiency" in your hen yard?

In the Campine fowl we have today the most efficient! Because she produces a large white egg at a minimum cost, and plenty of them; being non-setters, they appeal to all breeders, especially the small back yard man, as well as large breeders. The demand today is not a boom, or bubble ready to burst, because once they are in your yards, and—as the saying goes—"the proof of the pudding is in the eating," you will have no other breed.

You hear a few say the Campine will last a few years, then—"?." But to these people let me say, you are in error if you don't know what a Campine will do. Don't criticise them—"Get a few," and eat the pudding; you will not have to have sauce to make it palatable, so I repeat—"those of you who are from Missouri—GET A FEW."

You can read about egg records, cost of feeding, health, stability, etc., but the Campines lead them all. Try a few, make them prove to you their worth, and it will not be long before you will not be satisfied with a few.

I am receiving orders every day—"Repeats"—as well as new enthusiasts who are giving the Campine a trial. Those of you who are thinking of entering into the poultry business either from a "fancier's standpoint," or from the commercial "Hard Dollar" end, I repeat—"Get a few," and make them prove their worth.

THE GREATEST GOLDEN CAMPINE PEN EVER SHOWN IN AMERICA—FIRST at MADISON SQ. GARDEN—BOSTON and BALTIMORE 1913-14. E.F. DEAN, WILLIAMSPORT, PA.

A picture can hardly portray the beauty of the Golden Campine color. The rare combination of rich golden and greenish black markings has to be seen to be appreciated. In addition to the splendid markings and correct shades of color, the specimens in the above pen possess fine type and style. It was probably the best exhibition pen of the variety that has been shown in America. E. F. Dean, of Williamsport, Pa., is the fortunate owner of this splendid pen. The Golden variety is very vigorous and hardy, the chicks are thrifty and mature early, many pullets laying when they are less than five months old.—Wm. C. Denny.

Making a Start in Campines

The Selection of a Reliable Breeder From Whom the Purchase is to be Made—The Best Way to Start is Through the Purchase of Breeding Stock Rather Than Eggs or Baby Chicks—Extraordinary Results From a Pair of Birds—Do not Buy Small Birds With the Thought That They Will Mature—Insist on Getting Good Individual Quality

By E. F. Dean, Williamsport, Penna.

THE matter of selecting a breed or variety and the securing of stock of that kind is really a very important problem and the intelligent selection must be based upon a general knowledge of breeds and varieties. If this knowledge is not personal the assistance of some reliable poultryman should be solicited. After the breed has been decided upon the selection of stock of the kind desired would be a very simple matter if all stock of the kind selected were of the same quality, but, since this is not the case, the selection of stock often becomes a most perplexing matter on account of the variance in quality of that of the different breeders. It may, in order to obtain just what is wanted, be necessary to make purchase from various sources, discarding or returning that which is found to be not to your liking.

The purchase of stock of the variety selected should be with the idea of quality, health and vigor, as these three things are absolutely essential if results are to be secured. If absolutely a novice I would advise the purchase of the best trio you can afford and in one breeding season you can with care successfully raise to maturity many more birds than one would imagine. For instance, a number of years ago I purchased one cockerel and one hen (Buff Orpingtons) from one of the leading breeders, for which I paid as I then thought, an exorbitant price ($75), but after the breeding season was over I took an inventory and found that I had successfully raised 106 chicks. The undesirables were disposed of at the market at prices ranging from sixty cents to one dollar and a quarter each and even then I had more than I cared to winter over and disposed of a number at prices from $3 to $5 each and found that I had recovered my purchase price and a nice little sum toward the feed, beside having a fine flock of thirty birds to start with the next season. This is my own personal experience and I have little doubt that there are others who have done even better.

Now I will make a few statements as to why I have "Stuck to Campines." I have been an ardent admirer of this wonderful variety and not blindly as I have bred all varieties of Leghorns, Buff Orpingtons, Dark Cornish and two varieties of Rocks, not only before breeding the Campines but during this time. Two of the above varieties may now be found in my yards for sentimental reason only. Now, the Campine possesses all the qualities of egg production that have ever been known to any other variety, the eggs being large, pure white and very numerous. As a table fowl they are unsurpassed, having a full breast, resembling that of a pheasant to a very great extent. They mature very quickly and on very little feed, in fact I do not believe Campines have an equal in this respect. In comparison with other varieties in actual tests the results are remarkable, in fact, I am at a loss to know where they get what they make the eggs out of. This same condition exists in growing the young, they seem to thrive on practically nothing.

Now let us forget the financial advantages and go to the "fancy," as our English brothers call it. The beauty of the Campines is without comparison and they are not only beautiful but attractive—two qualities that do not always come together. You will have to admit that Campines are beautiful after looking over the illustrations in this book, so it is not necessary for me to elaborate further on this subject. If a man has a fancy he does not want that fancy to be easy, for if such is the case he will become careless and the work will become monotonous and it will cease to be a fancy. Not so with breeding Campines—if you are breeding as a fancy or for business you have a lot to study.

In this part of the chicken business I take the greatest pleasure and interest. It is indeed a study. Often I spend weeks studying my matings before actually mating for certain results and I seldom go wrong. I do not want to lead you believe that every specimen produced from the mating is what was expected, but that I seldom fail to get what I mated for.

Now in closing I would advise the greatest care in selection of stock and in purchasing same let your wants be known to the breeder from whom you purchase, that is, tell him whether you want birds from which to breed females of exhibition quality or males of exhibition quality, or birds of both sexes.

Be sure that the birds which you purchase for breeding have a sound undercolor and that their backs are clear. (Absolutely hen colored).

Do not purchase a male bird with a large unsightly comb, unless he has so many other good qualities that this defect may be overlooked.

Purchase birds of good size and weight, with good long backs. Do not let a breeder tell you that he has some birds of late hatch which will grow to be wonders, as nine times out of ten the birds which he is offering you are weaklings from the flocks hatched in regular breeding season. In other words, purchase fully matured stock and you will see at once what you are depending upon and your chances for success are much greater.

Do not buy day-old chicks.

The most satisfactory way to go into the chicken business is to purchase a pair or trio and not more than a pen of one male and six females, and by so doing you will grow with the chickens and you can give both old and young the necessary individual attention and you will know their every wish and each bird will know you.

If you have $100 to put into chickens, you have $25 more to go and see what you are going to get for that money and any honest poultryman will be tickled to death with this method of doing business.

You can not go wrong if you select Campines for your yards and are careful in the selection of your foundation stock.

Breeders Must Look to Health and Vigor

Breed for Vigor as Well as Show Points — Imported Birds Because of the Long Journey in Coops and the Changed Climatic Conditions, Are Not as Satisfactory as American Bred Birds — American Bred Birds Possess Wonderful Vitality as Shown by a Hatch of 60 Chickens From 60 Eggs, Set Under 4 Hens — Campine Eggs in Demand by the Public

By Walter C. Young, Pittsburgh, Pa.

AFTER visiting and showing Silver and Golden Campines at several of the largest shows last season, I became convinced that the Campines are fast becoming popular with the American fanciers. As I studied the winning specimens last season I was astonished at the wonderful progress the breeders have attained during the past few years. The Campines made a profound impression upon the breeders and the visiting public at the Club Show in Philadelphia and at Madison Square Garden, December, 1913. In fact, they made many friends and admirers, for they are such a sprightly, stylish appearing fowl. However, after all the popularity this fowl has enjoyed there is an under current of prejudice and criticism abroad among breeders and fanciers of the feathered tribe that the Campine is too delicate a fowl to last long in America.

Now, as a breeder and fancier of the Campine, I propose to point out in this article where we breeders are liable to make mistakes along the line of our breeding stock, in fact, a great many have already reaped dissatisfaction and became discouraged with the Campines.

FIRST PRIZE COCKEREL MADISON SQUARE GARDEN, DEC. 1913
SHENLEY HEIGHTS POULTRY FARM, PITTSBURG, PENN.

The 1st prize cockerel at the Madison Square Garden, N. Y., Show of Dec., 1913, was a cockerel possessing vitality that is truly remarkable—a quality that every Campine breeder seeks to establish in his strain. His penciling is exceedingly regular and clear from end to end.—F. L. Sewell.

In the first place, the all important factors of any breed are stamina and vigor, and it is just here that the Campine is being criticized today. This being so, it is up to us as breeders to improve upon the physical condition of our favorites. We all are aware of the fact that a great many Campines are lacking in stamina and vigor. This is true of the imported birds, no doubt due to the distance of travel and the difference in climatic conditions. I have found to my sorrow that the imported birds do not possess the same vitality our American bred birds do. I have imported and bought imported birds and found to my sorrow that they will not produce such strong, healthy, vigorous chicks as do our home bred birds. I have imported show specimens and exhibited and I must say they will not hold up in vitality. Let me say right here to the beginner who is starting in with the Campines and is contemplating importing his birds, either for breeding or exhibition purposes, that he will have considerable trouble and disappointment with the vitality of said birds, also with the fertility of eggs for hatching and the stamina and vigor of the chicks. I do say that a specimen that has been imported for exhibition purposes should not enter into the breeding pen during the year of importation.

Now, dear breeder, if you desire to build up a strain of strong, virile Campines, be very careful in the selection of your breeders at the start. I have met some who have become discouraged and have completely given up this variety and the fault was entirely with themselves and not with the breed. I know there is a desire on the part of us breeders to secure the very best specimens possible and many of us have purchased the winners at the largest shows in England and put them in our best shows and after the show season is over we found that our favorite birds were beginning to lack in vitality and would not fertilize the eggs. How in the world can we expect anything different after a bird has been shown all over England, then takes a long journey here; then resting possibly a week or a month, is shown at our leading exhibitions? When we stop to consider the endurability of a chicken one cannot expect such birds to be fit for breeding purposes.

I do not in any way desire to cast any reflection upon our good English breeders, for some of the best Campines to date have been bred there, but I do say with all honesty, that if we desire to import birds to improve our flocks, these birds should never be exhibited if they are to enter the breeding pens. I am putting forth this argument in defense of the breed here in America, for if our fanciers had not improved the physical side of the Campine we could never have hoped for an increased demand for this beautiful and profitable fowl.

To prove that the Campine does possess wonderful vitality, equal to any other variety of fowl, let me give a personal illustration : Last season I showed our Silver Campine cock at six of the largest shows a week at a time and afterwards put him in our best mating and secured 80 per cent to 95 per cent fertility and on four sets secured fifteen strong, vigorous chicks from fifteen eggs. At this time Mr. Denny, of Buffalo, visited our farm and to quote his words: "I never expected to see the old bird alive after being shown so many times." Now, I consider this goes to prove that by careful selection and breeding the Campines will have stamina and vigor the equal of any fowl in existence. It is up to the American Campine Club to educate our breeders to build up the vitality of this breed. I think it a good plan to get every breeder to state in his mating list whether the specimens in the different matings are home bred or imported, and in doing this I believe we shall win more admirers and breeders to the Campines.

We breeders hear at the shows that the Campines will not make good, for they lack vitality. Of course they will not in the hands of some breeders, but to the true, careful breeder who studies the Campine characteristics, success is assured and as soon as we Campine breeders wake up just so soon will the Campines become one of the popular breeds of the country.

The Campine is and can be made a great producer of large white eggs, eggs that command the attention of everybody when placed on exhibition. In our store here I have placed a basket of Campine eggs alongside of other white eggs and I have had customers select the Campine eggs in preference to the others. I can sell their eggs with ease, as their snow white appearance attracts the people. I believe there will be a large demand for eggs from this variety, as they possess a very fine flavor when cooked and are very palatable. Let us build up the commercial side of the Campine as an egg producer, for the demand is great for the large snow white eggs.

In order to become successful with the Campines you must get them acclimatised and breed only from strong, vigorous, virile specimens, and soon all this talk regarding the Campine as a delicate breed will be forgotten.

The Last Two Years With Silver Campines

The Pullets Lay in Winter, But the Hens That Lay in the Spring Produce the Best Eggs for Hatching Purposes—Caponized 50 Cockerels—Spraying for Lice—Splendid Winter Egg Production—Using the Hogan System

By W. H. Bushell, David City, Nebr.

I HAVE been breeding Silver Campines three years now and have given up my old business of brick manufacturing and am devoting all my time to breeding up a strain of Campines for show and utility purposes.

Before taking up the Silver Campine I read an article in the R. P. J. by Mrs. Van Schelle and I have proved what she wrote in regard to their laying qualities as hens up to five years old. Last January I mated up a pen of hens from three to four years old. They are the hens I imported for my foundation stock. Those nine hens laid almost equal to the yearling pullets, in fact, in the month of May I got more eggs from them then I did from pullet pens of equal numbers. The pullets laid best in the winter. From now on I shall use hens altogether in my breeding yards, as I find the hens will lay the eggs and they hatch good strong chicks.

In the season of 1913 I hatched out five hundred chicks. The cull cockerels I fattened and shipped to Omaha. I caponized fifty late hatched cockerels for our winter meat and they surely were fine eating—as good as turkey. I raised sixty of the best cockerels for my shipping trade and one won second prize at the Chicago Show in the hottest competition. I raised two hundred and fifty pullets and did not have a sick bird all season.

I did not raise one louse nor mite, nor have I seen a louse or mite on any of my birds up to this time. I spray my laying houses in July or August and the brooder house and colony houses in the winter when they are empty with rex lime sulphur mixture, the same strength as is used to spray fruit trees. I use a hand spray pump and plenty of spray to wet everything well and the one spraying in a year is all I use, but it did the work.

My last winter egg record was as good as I ever got from my Buff Orpingtons. To tell you of just two instances to prove what I say. On January 24th a party came to my place to buy a pen of Campines. I was showing him through the houses when we came to a pen of thirty March hatched pullets that I picked out and housed November 1st for winter eggs as a test pen, because in my business of shipping all winter I like to have a pen I do not have to cut into, for if you do you cannot tell anything about what they are doing. He said: "Is this pen laying? They look like they are." I told him, "Yes, they are laying from twelve to eighteen eggs every day. Is that not pretty good for this cold weather?" He said, "I guess it is, as I have over two hundred pullets (White Leghorns) and do not get that many eggs from all mine." Another breeder of some fame made a visit one evening in February just as I was starting to feed and gather the eggs; he followed me the rounds and when I was through he said, "I have gathered eggs for years in the winter, both Rocks and Leghorns, but this beats all the egg gathering I ever saw for winter from the same number of hens."

In mating up my breeding yards this winter I used the Hogan system. I felt sure I would find most all my old hens would go two hundred eggs or more by the way they had laid the two years I had them. I went over them and found all but one that was good for two hundred eggs. I cut the one out and ate her and sure enough she did not have many eggs in her. I picked out one pen of pullets that would go from two hundred to two fifty eggs by the Hogan system and they are proving it by the number of eggs I get from them. It is a comfort to gather eggs from such birds.

Four weeks ago last Saturday I took off a hatch of 115 chicks from 150 eggs and I moved them to different quarters. Last Saturday I caught them one at a time and counted them. I had just 112 chicks. That proves they are easily raised. I have about 500 young chicks and two incubators to hatch yet. I had just tested out one machine of 180 eggs and cut out six eggs. This is June 2nd. Pretty good for fertility from birds that laid all winter and they are still laying. Just as well as they have at any time. Last fall they laid splendidly up to moulting time until they were about naked.

We have a good climate for poultry here in Nebraska. We get lots of sunshine, not many cloudy days but just about rain enough to get good crops. We get some heavy storms in winter and it is pretty cold at times, but it only lasts a day or two at a time, then the sun comes out and warms up clear. We also have cheap feed, as we are in the winter wheat and corn belt, and Omaha is a good market just about like Chicago, according to the market reports.

My laying houses are partly on the open front order, but not to the extreme. Our wind is pretty thin and cold and it penetrates in the winter. I have tried tne Campines three winters now under confinement as winter layers, and I find them the equal of the Buff Orpingtons. After they are housed a week they do fine. They are easily handled and become quite tame.

Crystal Palace, London, where the greatest English Poultry Shows are held.

The History of the English Campine

This Article, Reprinted From "The Illustrated Poultry Record," London, Deals With the Early History of the English Type—The Important Question of Hamburg Crossing Discussed

By William W. Broomhead, England

THERE can be little doubt that the Campine is once more on the boom; and as a result there appears to be some friction among those fanciers who are keenly interested in it. Therefore, it behooves admirers of this charming breed to look carefully into matters. It will be remembered that in the March issue of "The Illustrated Poultry Record" I gave one side of the question by quoting from some remarks on the Campines exhibited at last year's Crystal Palace Show. It was a criticism on the English type that appeared in Chasse et Peche, from the pen of a Belgian expert, one Mr. Pulinckx-Eeman, who among other things, stated that he noticed "the introduction of Leghorn and Hamburg blood" into our strains. Hence in fairness to those English fanciers who have the welfare of the bird at heart, it will be as well if the other side is placed before readers. From correspondence I have had with the honorable secretary of the Campine Club, I cannot help arriving at his conclusion that the Belgian attack was nothing short of an advertising dodge. The crux is, the Campine is being taken up again with renewed vigor in America, and the Belgian breeders want the American fanciers to apply direct for birds. Reading between the lines it is not difficult to see that the continental breeders are jealous of our success, and being no fancy breed-ers they cannot appreciate why the English type succeeds in the show pen while the Belgian is an utter failure. The authority in question calmly puts it down to the solidity of the English speaking races, and while willingly handing America and England over to us, he urges his fellow countrymen to be in other lands before the English get a foothold. Apparently he thinks it impertinence of English fanciers to alter the breed, and so he with others has determined to make a serious attack on the breed in order to see if the Belgian type cannot take the place of ours, although at the same time continental breeders are covertly following our lead. This may be putting the English side of the question in strong light. Nevertheless, I think that occasion demands it.

In the Way of History

In England the Campine was introduced in 1898 or 1899 and it immediately became very popular; but a decline set in about 1903 or 1904, so that in 1905 the membership of the club had fallen from seventy odd to fifteen or sixteen. The history of the breed in America may be briefly stated. The Campine was admitted to the standards of the American Poultry Association about 1893—but at the next revision, five years after—

the A. P. A. standards are revised every five years—it was taken out. There is generally a good reason for such declines as these. In the present instance the English and American fanciers did not like the Belgian type of male, and the want of good markings, etc., which is demanded in any breed by them, was the cause of the decline. Double mating had to be resorted to to breed good cockerels and good pullets, according to the Belgian standard, and the result was evidently not worth the trouble. The English Club then decided that it was not desirable that Campines should require double mating, hence members decided to standardize the male bird similar to the female, which change took place at the beginning of the last decade. They did not, however, succeed in producing a standard specimen until 1904, which male bird was awarded first prize and cup by Dr. J. C. Gardner, at the Grand International Show at the Alexandra Palace. By the way it is interesting to note the history of this cockerel. Messrs. Parker Bros., I think, exchanged a sitting of Buff Orpington eggs for one of Campines with M. Oscar Thomaes, of Renaix, Belgium. This bird was hatched out of that setting and exhibited at Kendal, where however, he failed to catch the judge's eye, and returned cardless. At that Westmoreland Show, Mr. Wilson bought the cockerel and penned him, at the Alexandra Palace as above stated, while at the International the following year (1905) the same fancier exhibited that bird and some of his sons and won right along the line.

A Question of Crossing

The showing of this cockerel aroused something of a controversy, and it was asked, "How was he produced?" Was he the result of a cross with the Hamburg? This could hardly be so, since other fanciers would have had similar birds at the same time. From about 1900 onwards, the Campine was in the hands of some of the best English breeders, and had the Hamburg cross been of service it is a certainty that a cockerel would have been exhibited before 1904. One authority, a Hamburg specialist, said that he knew of Campine breeders, who had been supplied with Hamburg cockerels; but if so the produce was not forthcoming in the show pen. On this point the Rev. E. Lewis Jones, who has had more to do with the Campine than has any other fancier in this country, was most emphatic when I sought his opinion. "I know of none" he says. "'I have tried it and failed to get any useful result. I think probably if the cockerel was not the outcome of selection, then it was due to Holland-aishe, or what Mme. Van Schelle calls Friese." Admitted it is easy to say that the Hamburg was crossed in, because of the similarity of markings; but the usual result of such a cross is an equal band of black and white, both about as broad as a normal black bar on a Campine, and giving the bird a hooped appearance. On the Campine, however, the marking is a black bar, as near as possible three times as wide as the white ground color, this latter being open and bold and not like narrow threads. Of course there can be no doubt that the two breeds have something in common, since the Campine was the origin of the Hamburg, and the breeding of Campines on scientific lines could lead to the production of the Hamburg, since the tendency is the same way. Leghorn blood was mentioned by M. Pulinckx-Eeman. Now the only variety suggesting itself is the Cuckoo, but it has too many complications for anyone to give it serious consideration in connection with the Campine. Mr. Jones tells me that he has no horror of crossing and would not hesitate if he thought he could improve that way. "But," he adds, "all my attempts at crossing have yielded negative results. I firmly believe if the Hamburg cross was useful, Belgians would not bother to buy selling class birds at the Palace." The upshot appears to be that now the English breeders have brought the Campine to its present state of perfection and made it a popular fowl they are attacked. The Belgians would say "This popular breed is no Campine. The Belgian is the pure." They want the whole of the trade. That is the thing in a nutshell. But the English and American fanciers have deliberately discarded the Belgian type.

Interior view of Madison Square Garden, N. Y., the representative show of America.

FIRST PRIZE EXHIBITION PEN, MADISON SQUARE GARDEN, NEW YORK, DEC. 1913. M. R. JACOBUS, RIDGEFIELD, N. J.

No one in America deserves to have greater success with Campines than M. R. Jacobus, of Ridgefield, N. J., on account of his valuable pioneer work in exhibiting the good qualities of the breed. Mr. Jacobus, several years ago made a number of importations of the different types in order to experiment with them and know which were the most dependable in the breeding pen and the most reliable producers. These early importations and experiments were costly. American Campine breeders owe Mr. Jacobus a great debt for his splendid exhibits of eggs at the New York and Boston shows that for several seasons won against all exhibits in their class and proved the possibilities of the breed and won for it many champions. The Campine has brought competition and awakened new interest in breeds that produce beautiful, white-shelled eggs. We have added a class of birds to our exhibitions that are charming in style and fascinating in the regular contrasting bars of black and white, in the Silver variety and black and gold in the Goldens. The above group of Mr. Jacobus' first prize exhibition pen at the 1913 Madison Square Garden, New York, show, gives an idea of how charming the Campines can appear in the open where they can forage for most of their living. Mr. Jacobus breeds a strain of show quality Campines that are famous also for producing generous quantities of show quality white eggs. His Campines have won a great many prizes during the past six years at the New York and Boston shows.—F. L. Sewell.

History and Progress of Campines in America

The Exhibit of Belgian Campines at New York in 1894—The Breed Dropped From the Standard of Perfection
—The First Importation of the English Type Was in 1907—These Birds Were Then Exhibited as
"Improved Campines" — The Merits of This New Type—These Utility Features Must
be Preserved and Developed Since the Popularity of the Breed is
Based on Its Real Worth as Well as Its Beauty

By M. R. Jacobus, Ridgefield., N. J.

"IN THIS article treating on the Campines since they came to America, I will not attempt to get into ancient history of the breed abroad, but will confine myself to the breed as sent us and its growth and progress since it has been imported into America from both Belgium and England.

I will take my readers back a few years to 1893, when the breed was first imported from Belgium, its native home, into America and exhibited the following year, 1894, at Madison Square Garden, New York, at which show there were on exhibition two pens of the Belgian type birds; one being a pen of Silvers and the other a pen of Goldens. These birds as exhibited at that time were practically the same as the present-day Belgian type Campines.

On account of being what could be called a curiosity at that time, these two pens of birds attracted quite some attention. The exhibit, however, failed to produce much true interest in the breed, although behind it were some of the best fanciers of our country.

At that time I was breeding among other breeds, Golden and Silver Penciled Hamburgs, and I recall very clearly as I looked upon the exhibit of Belgian Campines that the appearance of these birds made such a poor impression upon me that I then remarked, "I would never breed those things." Little did I then dream that the appearance of the breed would be so improved as to permit me to become as deeply interested in it as I am at the present day.

The fanciers that were back of the Belgian type at the time they were originally exhibited at Madison Square Garden, New York, made efforts to popularize the breed. Through their efforts a Standard for both the Golden and Silver varieties was accepted by the American Poultry Association and admitted to the American Standard of Perfection. The Standard as then adopted called for what is practically the Belgian type of today.

On account of the appearance of the birds and the fact that to breed to such a Standard required a double mating, this Belgian type did not appeal to the public or the fanciers in particular, and as the birds apparently did not give sufficient results to induce the breeders to continue to handle them for their utility, the little interest that was aroused in this Belgian type soon died away, and the breed was finally dropped from the Standard of Perfection.

Introduction of the English Type

This was such a blow to the Belgian Campines that the Campines remained a dead issue in America until the English produced in the Silver variety, what is known as the English type, the males of the English type being marked, as is now well known, the same as the females and not having a white back and saddle, as in the Belgian type.

In the latter part of 1906 I sent an order to England for my first importation of Campines. At that time I did not put any faith in the Campines as a breed in themselves, on account of the poor showing made by the Belgian birds as imported years previously.

I imported these first Campines to use in a cross as an aid in producing a new breed I was then working on.

This shipment of Campines left England January 1st, 1907. When these birds arrived, I was surprised to find that they were of such a type as could be bred from a single mating and that by careful breeding, they could be much improved in their handsome markings.

As I had been a fancier of the Penciled Hamburgs for years, the markings of these English type Campines, which were similar in many ways to the markings of the Penciled Hamburg females, appealed to me.

In addition to this, the original hen which was sent me laid an exceptionally large, pure white egg. This large white egg I will admit here, as I have often done before, did more in attracting me to the Campines than their handsome markings.

When I discovered what improvements had been made in Campines by the English after the Belgian type had been discarded by American breeders shortly after they had been exhibited in 1894, I was so impressed with this new Campine that I decided to give them a trial; however, I did not exhibit them until I had tested them and proved to my own satisfaction that they were a worthy breed, that should be widely introduced into America.

When I first exhibited and advertised this new type of Campines (English type), I called them the "Improved Campine." This I did for the reason that they were so much improved over the Belgian birds exhibited in 1894.

As other breeders took up this new type of Campines and realized the advancement made, many of them were quick to adopt the name "Improved Campines," which was soon established, and by it the new type is now known in America.

My original importation of Campines being so promising, I at once sent back to England for more Campines and shortly afterwards imported some Belgian birds for comparison. While the original English birds were far superior to the Belgian birds, there were some changes necessary to be made in the English type to improve their beauty as well as change to be made so that they would give the very best results in this country.

To secure the best results in fertility and stamina in the offspring from these imported birds as breeders, it was of course necessary to thoroughly acclimate the stock. This was easily accomplished, however, in most cases in two generations.

Improvement of the Type in American Yards

The original English birds as imported, while very much improved in markings over the Belgian birds, lacked the distinct and well defined markings of our Campines of today. The head points in particular were also very poor, mostly all having poor combs, which were large and beefy. In the males the tails were short, practically devoid of markings, and carried very high, in many cases squirrel.

Since the original importations of the improved type, great strides have been made in the color and markings by both American and English breeders. Also many birds are now exhibited with tails much longer and carried at a low angle, as well as being handsomely marked.

The head is another section that has been much improved, as we now find some birds with combs that would be an honor to any breed.

The original birds varied considerably in shape or type; most of them being either too short in body or if they had ample length, the body was too broad, resembling or approaching the heavy Belgian Braekel. Having bred the Golden and Silver Penciled Hamburgs for over twenty years, I knew the necessity of keeping away from the short bodied bird, even if such is full of activity, when birds of stamina are desired, and it did not take me long to discover that the birds with great width of body, even if they had the length, were not active enough to be of any practical use in competition with the egg producing breeds of America.

Because of desiring to produce only birds of stamina, that were full of activity, I began to breed for a long narrow bodied bird, as I found birds of this type were the ones that retain their activity and stand the condition of our climate best.

The activity of such birds means egg production; and their shape, large eggs, such as have been exhibited at Boston, where they won in competition. I have often noticed birds of this type out over the fields busily engaged in search of food during unpleasant weather, while the broad bodied birds of the Braekel type would be in their coop or huddled back of some wind break.

Formation of a Campine Club

Knowing these conditions and personally being unable to advise the breeders as widely as should be done, I saw the necessity and therefore advised the formation of an American Campine Club, so breeders could decide and champion the type of birds best fitted for conditions in America. Before the formation of the American Campine Club, which was organized in 1911, there were many types of Campines being imported into America for which American breeders were sending good money abroad and in many instances receiving birds that were of little use for show or utility purposes.

Before the formation of the American Campine Club the name "CAMPINES" was not even thoroughly established in America. Some breeders called the Campines "BRAEKEL;" others desired to have them called "BRAEKEL-CAMPINES," and some were advertising Campines and selling instead genuine Belgian Braekel.

Many Belgian Braekels were being imported by Americans, who believed they were all that could be desired in the Campine line. If this had continued, it would likely have been the means of discouraging the breeding of Campines, as was the case when the Belgian type was tried and discarded years previous.

Since the American Campine Club was organized, American breeders have been better posted as to what is required and especially since the club has adopted a standard, Americans, if they send abroad for stock, send a description of such birds as they wish to secure.

Golden Campines

Shortly after importing my first English type Silver Campines, I imported from England my first Golden Campines. At that time the English had hardly commenced the improvement of the Golden Campines, so my first importation from England was in reality the same as the Goldens of Belgium, the males having the red backs and saddles of the Belgian type.

The original Golden Campines imported did not have as good egg qualities as the Silvers. For this reason I did not at that time offer the Goldens to the American public. These qualities were so inferior to those of the Silvers that it has taken several years to produce a strain that fully equals the Silvers in whiteness and size of their eggs. In this strain I have also produced the so-called hen-feathered Golden male.

At the present writing, June, 1914, there is a pen of these Golden Campines entered in the Missouri Egg Laying Contest. One hen in this pen has laid 126 eggs in six months, which six months included the three winter months. I mention this to show what will likely be accomplished in the egg line by a little careful breeding of American breeders. The eggs laid by this pen of Golden Campines, during the first five months of this contest averaged in weight, 26.136 ounces per dozen. In addition, this strain has the fine white egg qualities of the Silvers.

Egg Production of Highest Importance

The fact that Campine eggs have won first prize at Boston for five shows in succession, competition open to eggs of all breeds, has caused American breeders to consider the egg qualities of the Campines.

For the Campines to continue to gain favor in America, it is important that the breeders do not overlook their good egg qualities and that they breed only birds of such a type as give the best results in stamina, activity and egg production.

If the Campine breeders do not overlook the above qualities in their endeavors to retain and improve the handsome markings of their birds, the Campine breed will continue to grow in popularity in this country as it has done for the past few years.

I have devoted much space to the egg qualities of the Campines for the reason that I feel that it is because of the good egg qualities of the breed that the Campines hold the high place they do with American breeders.

While American breeders demand egg qualities they also have an eye for beauty and the handsomer we make our Campines, as long as they contain the egg qualities, the larger will become the demand for them.

Not only have the Silvers been improved in their color and markings, but the Goldens have also been improved in this respect, as well as their egg qualities. The males of the original Goldens imported into this country were what are now known as the Belgian type. Since that time, as explained above, the Golden Campines have been improved until we now have the so-called hen-feathered Golden Campine male, as well as the hen-feathered Silver male.

The Campine, a Beautiful and Productive Fowl

If Considered Only on Its Exhibition Merits, the Campine Would Have Many Admirers—American Poultry Breeders Have Discovered That Its Beautiful Plumage Covers a Valuable Egg Producer—It is an Aristocrat in the Show Room and a Profit-payer on the Farm—Proper Campine Shape and Plumage—The Ideals and Standard Adopted Should Improve the Profitable Characteristics of This Breed—Watch Their Constant Foraging Habits.

By Franklane L. Sewell, Niles, Mich.

THE plumage of fowls has always been an object of admiration. Feathered forms have a peculiar fascination to the eye quite beyond description. When a beautiful form is dressed in feathers of rare pattern and charm of color, an object of beauty is attained that is always a delight.

If the Campine were considered only on its exhibition merits, many would admire it and fancy it as a gem among aristocratic fowls. There are thousands who, possessing the love of the beautiful and the symmetrical, and being imbued with a bit of the spirit of a creator, devote hours of doting and pleasant recreation to birds, what may be at first simple admiration kindling into enthusiastic interest as day after day they care for their birds, watching the objects of their fancy develop toward their ideals.

This beautiful pattern of Campine plumage that has been so nearly established as to enable fanciers to breed it to a standard, must be as ancient as it is persistent. It is truly a marvelous habit in nature that causes its color pigment to be deposited in drifts with a degree of regularity that can be more or less controlled or modified by intelligent breeding.

The American poultry world has discovered that the dress of the Campine covers a truly valuable egg producer—call them egg "machines" if you must, though I dislike to associate the word machine with a living creature. Faithful laying habits have gained for them in their native country the title of "Every day layers." In America, with its modern regard for mechanical efficiency, it is not surprising that they have been called "egg machines."

The most surprising part of Campine history is that British and American fanciers were so tardy in appreciating the possibilities of the combined beauty and profitableness possessed by the Campines. The unique form and style of plumage of the Campine presents an outline different from other breeds previously recognized in our American Standard of Perfection. For its small amount of bone, the breast is very broad and meated to unusually full proportions. Even with its short plumage the breast and body are so plump and the bird has such rounded curves that its type is emphatically distinguished as an aristocrat in the show room and a profit-payer on the farm. Added to this is the nervous temperament that characterizes all the greatest laying races and its apparently conscious pride.

The round, full eye of the Campine bespeaks nobility among fowls, set as it is in a face expressive with animation. On the full, rounded head rises the bright, crimson comb and below the beak and throat are suspended the quivering wattles, whose equally brilliant color lends gayety and contrast to the white ear lobes and silver white plumage of the throat and neck. Every line of the male reveals pent-up energy and vigor and in his mates the busy, thrifty temperament that turns the wheels of the "egg machinery" is evident.

Watch their constant foraging habits. See them search the leafy corners and mossy banks of the woodland, or scratch among the rough weeds and grasses of the field, or help to rid the pastures of the hoppers and crickets, the worms and slugs, the borers and cutworms. The pest infested gardens and orchards become more productive and the meadows greener where the active little Campines range in the proper seasons. You can tell a farm where the hens have helped to destroy its enemies.

Show Best When At Liberty

Those who see fowls only in the pens at our great poultry shows cannot appreciate half their beauty and charm. The very limited space of the show coops compels the birds to appear in attitudes, but few of which are graceful. During the show season they are much restricted in order to fit them for judging by arbitrary standards. Liberty, out where life is worth living, encourages a more vivacious spirit in these creatures that were created to earn their own livelihood, and they know even better how to do it than man, though he invents the best of "systems."

So let me remind you that the most interesting time to observe the true beauty and charm of the Campines is when they are enjoying their freedom, finding their own living along the hedge rows or on lands over which they are permitted to forage. At the end of the day, when the sun is low and an allowance of food calls the flocks about their roosting quarters, the finer qualities of show markings appear at close range. The beauty of the clear, precise markings that command top-most prices for exhibition purposes will appear on nearby inspection. Those very narrowest pencilings of white, popular as an extreme show room fashion, can be appreciated only when the bird is in hand or confined to close quarters.

Standard makers need not be reminded that the beautiful points of fowls should be readily observed out of hand and that the most fascinating times for poultry keeping is of longer duration than the show season, when birds are confined and subject to the close scrutiny of critics and of the few who have to use magnifying glasses to see the faults or comprehend the beauties of Standard-bred poultry. Fowls that depend upon microscopical examination for appreciation of their chief beauty cannot hope for a long lived popularity. Out of the great majority who profit by poultry keeping and egg production are to come many of the industry's best breeders. Fowls that excite admiration at first glance awaken most widespread interest among this great class and, providing the productive powers prove that the fowls are highly profitable to keep, their continued popularity is assured.

Beauty in the form of the Campine depends, as it does in the shape of all fowls, upon its symmetrical proportions and graceful contour of outline. Unbalanced proportions, lop-sided carriage or any degree of deformity that throws the bird out of balance offends even the untrained eye, although he may not be able to discover the cause of the awkwardness in the specimen.

With beauty in form or proportion will be combined those practical qualities for which most poultry keepers maintain their flocks of hens. With irregularity of form may be found unreliability in the qualities that should make the bird profitable. Those who keep poultry for profit have learned by expensive experience to avoid freaks and extravagant extremes.

The Campine form impresses the eye of an old poultry keeper as being full of common-sense hen values—of having the beauties of form that make little hens pay big profits.

There is a gamey fineness of bone and flesh with an apparent minimum of waste. When handled, one realizes their plumpness in every section and that the breast is broad for a bird of its size. There is a busy sprightliness of action that means that nothing will escape them that can be turned to account for their liveli-

hood and productiveness. These points of beauty in form and action are possessions of genuine value, especially when found in a fowl possessing interesting plumage.

The Plumage of the Campine

The rounded surface of the Campine's plump form present a most advantageous model over which to display plumage of sharply contrasted bars of color. When the Campine plumage is clear, strong, sharp and arranged in a pattern that presents a color scheme that is plain to the eye; when the birds move at a little distance where one can observe them as they feed about their attendant, an ideal in plumage is secured that exhibits truly practical beauty—a beauty that serves the purpose of making the bird charming to every lover of feathered life. The color arrangement of the barred plumage must possess great regularity in order to be most attractive.

Group I—Upper row; No. 1 is a typical Jones-Kennedy cockerel, winner of first at Madison Square Garden, New York, December, 1911. This bird has distinguished himself as a breeder in the yards of J. Fred N. Kennedy, Birch Cliff, Ontario. No. 2 is one of the originators of the "Green Sheen" strain, imported by Frank E. Hering, proprietor of The Willows Farm, South Bend, Ind. He is a cock bird and has dense black bars and wonderful green sheen. No. 3 is a very plump, full-bodied, well-matured cockerel that made a striking success at the early autumn shows of 1913, owned by Dr. J. H. Prudhomme, Thurmont, Md. No. 4 is a Jones-Kennedy cockerel of beautiful shape and extraordinary clear color, showing decided contrast in the black and white barring, with a neck hackle of rare purity. No. 5 was a first prize cockerel at Madison Square Garden, December, 31, 1912-January 4, 1913, owned by Manhattan Farms, Brighton, N. Y. No. 6 was a first prize cockerel at Madison Square Garden, December 26-31, 1913, owned by C. F. Rankin, proprietor Schenley Heights Poultry Farm, Pittsburg, Pa.—F. L. Sewell.

The majority of Campine fanciers have decided that at present the Standard barring on the body should be of black bars, four times the width of the white bars. No doubt this is the safest plan at the present period of Campine history. The gray in the black bar is most easily obliterated by this extreme dark plumage. When the plumage can be bred to show clear black and pure white, the temptation will not be so great for such an over-dose of the dark color, and with a lighter body plumage it will be more possible to obtain purer color in the much desired silver-white hackle.

On specimens possessing bars of absolute black (greenish glossy black) without a trace of any sooty gray admixture and with bars of pure white, unspotted by gray flecks, it will be found that even three times as much black as white gives us a sensationally bright plumage of undisputed beauty and with such a body plumage almost spotless hackles are possible. Cockerel No. 4 in Group I is an example of this type, one that is an unmistakable gem seen either close at hand in the show pen or at some distance. Fanciers of the

Wyandotte remember that their favorites went through a period when very dark plumage was fashionable and the reason for it was that gray was easily obliterated, especially in the first year's plumage. Later when gray could be more successfully bred out, the brighter, clearer, more plainly observed plumage proved to be the most valued. This may prove to be the history of the Campine and is worth keeping in mind by those who expect to make the most of the breed in the future.

After serious imperfections of shape, this gray in the plumage is one of the first defects to be criticised by exacting admirers of the breed. Judges will not tolerate it any more than they will eyes that are not typical of the breed in color, or "hackled" plumage. These three defects are in the class of blemishes that are apt to disqualify in good competition. Gray in the plumage is the most common color defect in the breed today and nothing more surely sets a bird outside of high-priced exhibition quality breeding stock. On farms where the production of eggs for market is the sole aim—where eggs sell for cents instead of dollars—such little fine

Group II—No. 7 is a Jones-Kennedy hen that won first at Madison Square Garden, December, 1911. Afterwards she contributed her strong breeding qualities to the yards of J. Fred N. Kennedy, Birch Cliff, Ontario. No. 8—A choice bright colored pullet from the yards of Dr. J. H. Prudhomme, Thurmont, Md., which was first at New York Fair, New York City, 1913. No. 9—A wonderfully clear colored pullet bred by Frank E. Hering, proprietor The Willows Farm, South Bend, Ind., winner of first at Chicago, December, 1913. No. 10 is a much admired pullet, winner of first prize at Madison Square Garden, New York, December, 1910, owned by M. R. Jacobus, Ridgefield, N. J. She is of the type recommended by Mr. Jacobus as particularly strong for egg production. The uniformity of barring and almost perfectly curved breast line are among this pullet's unusually strong breeding and show points. Mr. Jacobus has always placed egg production first of all qualities in his Campines. No. 10 and No. 12 are types from his yards that he points to particularly as illustrating the egg laying type, No. 12 being from his first prize Madison Square Garden exhibition pen, December, 1913. No. 11 is a type of Jones-Kennedy pullet favored for breeding the highest class exhibition females in the yards of J. Fred N. Kennedy, Birch Cliff, Ontario.—F. L. Sewell.

points of fancy color mean no more than the color of the hair on a Jersey cow's tail. The black and white bars on the Campine will always be the feature in gilt-edge show birds that can command the top-most prices.

The Shape of the Campine

With the prevailing fashion demanding low-carried tails in so many Standard breeds, the Campines that have upright tails are not those that are considered the most beautiful, although too many Campines that have appeared in the show room have had these upright tails. In poses, such as portrayed in the three upper males, Nos. 1, 2 and 3 in Group I, the tails are carried in pleasing symmetry with the remaining sections of the

type, being distinctly in a class by itself. (Note—Attention is called to the footnotes written by Mr. Sewell for the cuts which he made especially for this article.—Ed.)

Description of Illustrations

In some specimens of the Campines there appears a spirit of over-anxious pride (common in Bantams), as if making a ridiculous attempt to appear great. No. 13 only moderately expresses the self-conceit that can appear in a bird of mediocre style. In this outline is illustrated the sharp angle formed by the abruptly sloping back and too high carried tail. Such an angle does not harmonize with the rounded form of the Campine. The carriage of this specimen's neck forms a curve too

Group III—These three outlines illustrate defects and variations seen in the Campine. No. 13 is a Campine male of over-proud carriage. The comb shows wrinkles and irregularities of serrations. The wattles are coarse and angular and not nicely rounded; the neck curves too much backward, the back is too sloping and the tail is too erect and is carried at too sharp an angle with the back. The wings are too round at the points and the legs are too much bent at the hocks. No. 14 is too slender, too narrow and shallow bodied and flat breasted for a high quality Campine. In No. 15 the comb is irregular, wrinkled in front over the nostrils and there are too many points, also a double point, the fourth from the front, and there are three instead of one point on the rear blade. Combs like this and No. 13 are too large and the rear blade of both is much too coarse and large and sags down on the rear of the head. The comb on No. 14 is much better.—F. L. Sewell.

birds. I should not favor a tail carried lower than that of No. 1 on a Campine, nor one higher than the tail of No. 3 I could not admire, because it would not be in keeping with the bird's type.

From the demand for birds with "a good, low-carried tail," one might imagine that this was the most important end of the bird and to be criticized first. However, this is not the case. The experienced judge views the bird first as an entire object, trying to decide on the most symmetrical individual for the premier place.

The carriage of the head is always of great importance in the beauty of any specimen, because on it depends the typical style and it also shows the intelligence of the bird. The head of the best Campine is not carried stretched up with straightened neck, but with the neck well arched back, combining a graceful opposite curve with the front line of the full rounded breast. No. 1, Group I, portrays a capital pose to illustrate this feature. A long neck with the moderately short tail of the Campine, would not be symmetrical. On the other hand, a neck that is a little too short is apt to present a type that would approach the fashion of the Dorking. With lines elongated in a bird of over size, the type approaches the Minorca, or if it is too slender, and small the style inclines toward the Hamburg. The Campine is unique and possesses a neat, plump beautiful

severe to be graceful. The arch is too pronounced and thrown backward too far. The points of the wings are carried very much too low. They should be held up neatly at the sides of the body, resting above the fluff of the second joint. With the back too slanting, the breast is also carried too upright, and this section, instead of being plump and rounded, shows lumpy and lacking full development.

Some of the faults common to large single combs are seen in this sketch—wrinkles, sometimes called "thumb marks," appear in the front over the nostrils; double points always an extremely severe blemish; loose texture and lopping points; split blade and both front and rear blades sagging too close to the beak and to the rear of head or neck; wattles that show angles instead of nicely curved edges. Other sections of the bird look lumpy, angular and irregular. Added to all these defects, the bird does not stand firmly on its feet. It turns in and bends too much at the hocks. This is an example of qualities opposite to those that Campine fanciers select when breeding for beauty in their birds. There are other characteristics that through indifferent breeding or crossing may spoil the type desired.

In No. 14 the outline shows a type of Campine that appears too flat on the breast and too slender throughout. It possesses a degree of pleasing style, but is quite foreign to what Campine experts agree is to be the Standard for the breed. It is not Leghorn, nor is it Hamburg, neither are its racy lines typical of the Campine. The true Campine can be a better fowl than the type toward which this bird's lines digress.

The temptation for greater size, longer back, lower tail and white lobes, if these be desirable, tempts the short cut through other races with its many disastrous results. Short cuts are risky (even if any rapid change could be conceived as a possible improvement) in the hands of any but old experienced breeders. The Campines in their purity are a truly wonderful race of fowls and any deviation from the genuine type should be regarded with suspicion, and if made at all, records of their breeding should be kept with the utmost caution. The outline of male No. 15 shows a large, coarse type, too long for its depth. The lines are too straight to be typical for a Campine. The head is too coarse and the size and drooping character of the lobes leads one immediately to suspect the use of the blood of a large Mediterranean, by which the economic habits and dependable blood lines of the profitable little Campine might easily be upset.

Another diversion from the proper type is seen in some exhibits of Campines, like No. 16, in which too much fluff points to coarseness of flesh. Fineness of flesh is a quality of considerable importance to be guarded in the Campine. The day is coming in America when quality as well as quantity is going to demand appreciative values. The length of plumage as well as quantity or fluff are both points to guard against. With added length of plumage will appear hackled saddle feathers, which would ruin the beauty of a Campine. Too much fluff will ruin the quality and the barring in the plumage. Moderate closeness of plumage is essential to the finest plumage and quality of barring. In No. 16 the surfaces are too flat and the

Fig. 16—Outline of a Campine male showing a form of body that is too coarse and clumsy, lacking the graceful carriage of the Campine race. The breast is too square and is not rounded as in typical specimens. The plumage is too abundant and fluffy and too long over the saddle.—F. L. Sewell.

lines forming the sections turn too squarely over bunches of fluff instead of rounding nicely over plump, fleshy portions, such as we find in the best type of Campines.

Campine Females

The illustrations forming the group of six Campine females tell better than any words how extraordinarily plump and well balanced representative specimens of this beautiful race can be. The last three years of Campine history have revealed to American fanciers qualities which they could not resist. The attractive qualities in the Campine hen are destined to establish her as a permanent institution on farms where fowls enjoy unrestricted liberty. Where poultry is kept on the extensive plan, I feel confident the Campine hen will prove a genuine success. The group of females shows six high-class show quality specimens representing the stock of four different breeders whose strains are among the foremost. The established beauties of the breed are clearly brought out in these specimens. Few breeds could show more distinct quality or more uniformity.

The round, full eye of the Campine hen is one of its strong, distinguishing characteristics. Its dark color, with dark eye lids and its sparkling high light add to its apparent size.

The ear-lobe of the Campine is bluish white and the truest of chalk white eggs may be expected. The more red there is in the ear-lobe the less we can depend on the fowl to produce white eggs.

Another point in favor of the Campines is their ability to produce eggs that are large at both ends, a feature that is given extra value by a number of leading Campine breeders. This quality is likely to create a special demand for the eggs and probably special prices will be paid. It will be noted that the oval form of the Campine body is similar to the shape of the symmetrical oval of their eggs. (See outline illustrations.)

Group IV—No. 17 shows the outline of a female that is too narrow and not deep enough to be typical. She is not smooth enough nor broad enough over the line of the shoulders and back and the tail joins the saddle in a clumsy style. Outline No. 18 shows a female very much wanting in breadth of hips and in depth and roundness of body and breast. The breast and body are almost V shaped in profile underneath. She is very deficient in what goes to make a Campine beautiful or profitable. The comb should not be erect, but should lop to one side. No. 19 shows a female that is over large and coarse and that is too loose or fluffy in plumage. This is a type too much inclined to make flesh, feathers and fat out of their food instead of turning it into eggs.—F. L. Sewell.

Some imported birds have not had the desired proportionate length of body that the American breeder favors and considers necessary to get the largest egg production. This is a matter that is not being overlooked and we find a number of breeders are particular to select and mate to produce the desired length of breast and body. Over-large size is not sought in the Campines by breeders who know the true purpose for which the breed is kept. It will be noted in the Club Standard of the breed that the greatest value is placed on the back and breast. The broad hips and the full, deep breast of the Campine hen have exceptional economic value and they truly excel in these sections. Breeders are determined, therefore, to preserve and, if possible, to improve them and to establish these exceptional values in the race.

The Club Standard for neck calls for "medium length." Its legs and toes are described as "rather long and slender." This does not mean that stilted shanks would look in harmony with Campine symmetry; on the other hand, very short legs give the fowl a waddling gait, do not look well and fail to help the ambitions of a good forager.

In hen No. 7 there is a splendidly developed body, carrying itself in queenly fashion with every line declaring thrifty activity in its temperament. The color is intensely black and white, all sections of the bird matching well. The bird is extraordinarily free from gray and the barring is strong and precise. The wing and tail are wonderfully well barred. Such color in a hen is very rare. In general proportions, length and depth of body and combination of back and tail, it would be difficult to improve her.

No. 8 in this pose exhibits a level body of unusual length. The comb drops jauntily, the legs would answer Club Standard description, the color is bright and in pleasing contrast. Such a type would be sought by those whose birds were too short and upstanding and would be valuable in correcting the over-smart carriage sometimes seen.

If one is looking for brilliant contrasts, his fancy will be pleased by the pullet illustrated as No. 9. Seldom does one find plumage with such flashy barring. It is regular, too, and shows well in wing secondaries and tail plumage, which are two of the most difficult sections on which to produce clear, strong bars free from gray. The breast, shoulders and back of this pullet exhibit lines of unusual roundness. The side plumage of the breast turns over the wing fronts in a remarkably smooth fashion. This has always been greatly admired in exhibition birds. In this pose her slant of back, also combination of back and tail, come very close to the popular ideal. This pullet was one of the best pullets bred in the United States last year.

One of the first things a Campinist notices when criticizing the type of his favorites is the balance of its body. They do not like to see the bird stand with the body too high up in front. They prefer to have the slope to the tail very moderate. After posing the pullet, No. 10, I asked its owner if it stood quite high enough in front, and he assured me that the Campine fanciers preferred them not stretched up in front, but rather moderate in slant and that this closely approached the desired pose of the body. This female has plenty of depth for a Campine in its first year, with sufficient length of breast. The neck is posed, perhaps, a trifle straight. The head, comb and wattles are neat. The carriage and spread of tail are very much to the liking of Campine fanciers.

No. 11 presents an unusually symmetrical type and the regularity in size and width of the bars adds to the even, harmonious effect caused by the regular distribution of color. Very few Campines match so well in all sections. The tail in this pose is dropped a little too low, which causes the break at the juncture of the back and tail. The oval form of the breast and body is easily observed in this pullet, and if the tail was at its most common height, there would hardly be an angle formed between any of the sections. The breast line from the throat to the thighs is one long, sweeping curve—a line that combines very practical beauty. The neat comb that sits pretty well up in front and lops only moderately, is probably the type of comb that will always prove popular on the Campine female. It gives the eye free vision and such a comb can be depended on not to produce over-sized combs on the males.

The broad hips and wide-set thighs, with well-filled body between the wings, seen on bird No. 12, would indicate a type with great egg laying capacity. This characteristic in the exhibition Campine should never be lost sight of. Narrow, pinched bodies that cannot afford room for egg making machinery, if allowed to win first honors, eventually would put the best laying breed into ill repute.

The Campine has been introduced into America by breeders who first of all have had the good business foresight to acquaint the public with the quality of the Campine's white eggs and the great quantities of them they produce at comparatively small cost. It is to be hoped that this valuable characteristic in the Campine will always be preserved and improved and that the beautiful barred plumage and symmetrical oval form of the Campine in the hands of our American breeders can always be accepted as indications not only of outward

Fig. 21—Outline of a prize Campine pullet, true to life, showing the oval form typical of the best specimens. The dotted V shaped lines show the form of a body deficient in value for table use or egg production, which is to be avoided.—F. L. Sewell.

Fig. 20—This Campine is not deep enough in body and appears too narrow and may look too long in proportion to be typical. However, the Campine sometimes produces individuals that may be too short. From this type the eggs are not up to the size that Campines are capable of producing. For this reason the short type will be discouraged by Campinists.—F. L. Sewell.

beauty, but of line-bred record layers and profit payers. Even those who are not specially attracted to them will have to admit that "handsome is as handsome does."

The Campine breeds comparatively true to type. However, there will be found some variations as in all breeds and these differences will indicate practical values as well as show room qualities. Precisely what certain outward characteristics signify in economic values, in most instances, are not yet thoroughly understood.

The trap-nest furnishes us evidence so that accurate records may be kept. Outward appearances sometimes have proved misleading, but when such a good practical form as the oval in the Campine is found to be always uniformly dependable as a producer of large quantities of eggs and is so recognized by the oldest breeders, Standard makers should deem the matter worthy of a good deal of consideration.

Champions of the Campine are earnestly working to make sure that the standards of Campine beauty follow along practical lines and that only those ideals are adopted that shall insure the genuine improvement of the profitable characteristic of the breed.

The Production of the English Type Gold Campine Male

While Golden Campines of the True English Type Were Produced in America by M. R. Jacobs, and in Belgium by Dr. Gommers, England Also Was Working on This New Variety—The English are the Greatest Color Breeders in the World and Their Golden Campines Acquired First Place—How the Matings Were Made That Produced the English Birds

By Rev. E. Lewis Jones, Knighton, Radnorshire, Eng.

THE history of the English type Silver Campine cockerel is well known to most Campine fanciers. For the benefit of new members it will he well very briefly to recapitulate it. The first English-type male seen in England sprang from a sitting of eggs imported by a firm of breeders in North of England, from M. Oscar Thomaes, of Renaix, Belgium, in 1904. It is admitted by Belgian breeders that this type of bird occasionally appears in their yards as a sport, so termed. But, although the bird is of pure Campine race, the Belgians have never bred from the hen-feathered male, being under the mistaken impression that "birds with this plumage are not virile;" and also because they prefer the white-topped cockerel, with long-flowing white saddle hackle. The bird above referred to was shown at the Kendal Show, and was bought by Mr. Wilson, of Penrith. He showed him at the Club Show, 1904, under Dr. Gardner, and got 1st and challenge cup. Prominent Campine fanciers all purchased sons of this bird, which is thus the direct ancestor of the English-type Silver Campine cockerel as known today in England and the States.

For some years the Campine variety was practically represented by the Silvers; the classes for Golds at the annual Club Show did not fill, and they were abandoned. Occasionally a single specimen was shown in the Silver classes at the Palace or Dairy—Mr. Mattock's pullet won the challenge cup over Silvers in 1906—but the variety was otherwise unrepresented in the show pens.

Meanwhile, two English breeders of this variety were busy attempting to produce a Golden male of the type of the Silver. As there were hardly any Gold Campines in England, birds were imported from Belgium. This importation checked experiments for some time—as the birds had to be acclimatised and a healthy strain to be established.

The honor of producing the first English type Gold cockerel belongs to Mr. E. S. Mattock, whose matings are given below. It will be noted that the Gold crossbred pullets when mated to Silver cockerels gave exactly the same results as given by the pure Gold pullets in the Heyope matings. Throughout the whole series of experiments it was immaterial whether cross-bred

Silver or pure Silver hens were used; whether cross-bred Gold or pure Gold hens were employed, the male bird was the determining factor.

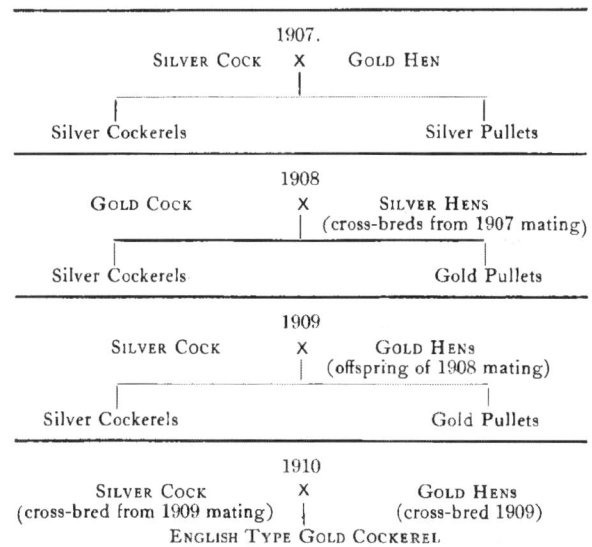

```
                        1907.
          SILVER COCK    X    GOLD HEN
                         |
          |                              |
    Silver Cockerels              Silver Pullets
--------------------------------------------------
                        1908
          GOLD COCK     X    SILVER HENS
                         |   (cross-breds from 1907 mating)
          |                              |
    Silver Cockerels              Gold Pullets
--------------------------------------------------
                        1909
         SILVER COCK    X    GOLD HENS
                         |   (offspring of 1908 mating)
          |                              |
    Silver Cockerels              Gold Pullets
--------------------------------------------------
                        1910
      SILVER COCK       X        GOLD HENS
 (cross-bred from 1909 mating) |  (cross-bred 1909)
          ENGLISH TYPE GOLD COCKEREL
```

Matings of Mr. E. S. Mattock to Produce English Type Gold Cockerel.

Mr. Mattock produced two English-type cockerels in 1910, and mated up one in 1911. Among the progeny were again two clear-back cockerels. Thus there were in 1911, counting Dr. Gommers' bird (of which more anon), five English-type Gold cockerels in existence. I did not know of any of these birds until August, 1911.

At this time my experiments had reached the stage when I had obtained the Silver cross-bred cockerels, which next season bred all the cockerels shown in 1912.

Before crossing Golds and Silvers two seasons had been wasted in foolishly trying to obtain the required bird by means of Hamburgh crossings. Our present knowledge shows that this cross is valueless, because there is no male bird (the determining factor) of the Gold-pencilled Hamburgh variety which possesses the requisite characteristics to produce our type of cockerel.

We believe that a certain pencilled Hamburgh breeder has conducted almost similar experiments with his varieties, but we have not examined any of his results.

The Series of Matings Which Produced the English-Type Gold Campine At Heyope Rectory

(a) The first experiment made was the crossing of a Gold Campine cock with a Silver hen. The result of this mating was disappointing—the cockerels were all Silvers of the Belgian type, the females all Gold. Next year one of these Silver cockerels was mated with the Gold pullets, his sisters.

(b) This pen produced Gold and Silver cockerels, Gold and Silver pullets; but the cockerels were all of the Belgian type. Clearly an English-type Gold male was not to be produced in this fashion, and two years' work had given no result.

(c) The same season, however. an English-type Silver male—an excellent breeder, sire of several Palace winners—was mated with pure Gold hens of best markings and type obtainable. The chickens from this mating were most vigorous, and were all reared to maturity. But again an impasse seemed to have been reached; for to all appearance both cockerels and pullets were pure Silver. The cockerels were all well-marked birds of English type—not a Belgian saddle-hackle feather among them.

The next step seemed to be the mating together of these Silver cross-breds in the hope of producing a Gold male in the next generation. But at this stage in the experiment it was observed that, so far, the results obtained were exactly parallel with those obtained by Messrs. Doncaster and Raynor in crosses made between two specimens of the Currant Moth—Abraxas Grossulariata and its variety, Laticolor—(c) a male grossulariata moth crossed with a female alticolor produced only grossulariata—both male and female, just as the Silver male and Golden female gave all Silver chickens.

FIRST PRIZE HEN, SHAPE & COLOR SPECIALS, MADISON SQ GARDEN, JANUARY, 1913. COCKEREL WINNER OF SECOND BOSTON, JAN. 1913.

The first English-type Campines were imported to America in 1907 by M. R. Jacobus, Ridgefield, New Jersey, and the first exhibits at the Madison Square Garden, New York, Show were made by Mr. Jacobus, who filled the classes with his Campines, although at that time there was no prize money to be won. Mr. Jacobus exhibited Campine eggs in the dressed poultry and egg section of the Boston Show, 1910, and that year, also in 1911, 1912, 1913 and 1914 won first prize for the whitest dozen of white shelled eggs. He was the founder, and since its organization, has been the efficient secretary of the American Campine Club. To him of all Americans, belongs the credit for the great strides in popularity that the Campine has taken, for he has been the Campine's greatest champion. Being a man of independent means, the opportunity to "cash in" on this new breed, did not take hold of Mr. Jacobus. He steadfastly refused to meet the demand by importing birds and selling them, or eggs from them, knowing full well that the stock was not acclimated to conditions in this country, and that a generation or two of breeding was necessary to fit them to their new environment. Again, after originating his own strain of Golden Campines, he declined to sell eggs for hatching until he had improved the egg qualities to the Silver Campine Standard.

When these cross-bred moths mated inter se, they produced (d) grossulariata males and grossulariata females; also laticolor females but no laticolor males. That is to say, if the experiment in Campines continued on analogous lines, the Silver (to all outward appearance) cross-bred chickens, mated together, would produce (d) Silver cockerels, Silver pullets and Gold pullets—but no Gold cockerels; and, as a matter of fact, when this mating was tried this is what happened. Thus in both reciprocal crosses—(a) Gold male and Silver female, and (c) Silver male and Gold female—the first generation chickens, when bred together, failed to produce in the next generation the Golden male required. The second generation from (a) gave (b) Gold cockerels, Belgian type, and the second generation from (c) failed to give in (d) any Gold males at all.

As a matter of fact, the English-type male was produced in the same year as the (d) generation just referred to—by following on the lines of Mr. Doncaster's experiments.

When these experiments with moths were first carried out, there were no males known of the laticolor variety. Pursuing his investigations, Mr. Doncaster mated together a grossulariata cross-bred male and a laticolor female. This union produced grossulariata males and females, and also laticolor males and females. These results determined the next mating for the production of the English-type Gold cockerel. Substitute Silver cockerel (offspring of Silver cock and Gold hen) for grossulariata cross-bred male, and Gold hen for laticolor female—then the offspring should be Silver cockerels and pullets and Gold cockerels and pullets. This was, in fact, the mating which produced the Gold cockerel, English type.

Below are given in tabular form the results of the various matings between the Silver and Golden varieties of the Campine fowl. Those who would further

trace the similarity between these and the matings of the two varieties of the Currant Moth, are referred to "Mendel's Principles of Heredity"—W. Bateson, pp. 174 to 177, and "Reports to the Evolution Committee of the Royal Society," No. 4.

English Type Gold Male Produced in Belgium

In the autumn of 1911, when traveling in Belgium, I visited the yards of Dr. Gommers of Meerle. Here I saw, among the birds bred that year, a Gold Campine cockerel, English type. Mme. Van Schelle, who accompanied me, purchased this bird. This was the sire of the winning birds shown by Mme. Van Schelle and Mr. R. Edwards, jun.

Dr. Gommers was unable to give me the pedigree of the bird; but he attributed it to the effect of the infusion of "Frise de la Hollande" blood. I quote from a letter recently received from him:

"L'origine (du coquelet) n'est pas tres claire. Il y avait dans mon parquet:

(1) Un coq. Campine dore belge.
(2) 1 poulette frise doree.
(3) 1 poule provenant de
      Coq. Hambourg dore a plumage de poule
      et de poule Campine doree.
(4) quelques poules doreses.

Je ne saurais dire au juste la provenance, je suppose de la poule Frise, vu que le pere de cette poule etait aussi a plumage de poule."

I know, from experiments carried on in the autumn of 1912, that this is a possible mode of production. I imported from Dr. Gommers two cockerels—Silver and Gold—Frise de la Hollande. Mated with Campine pullets of their own color, they produced English and Belgian-type cockerels. As soon as we were satisfied that clear-backed males could be thus produced, we potted them. They were useless for breeding-in, as they were

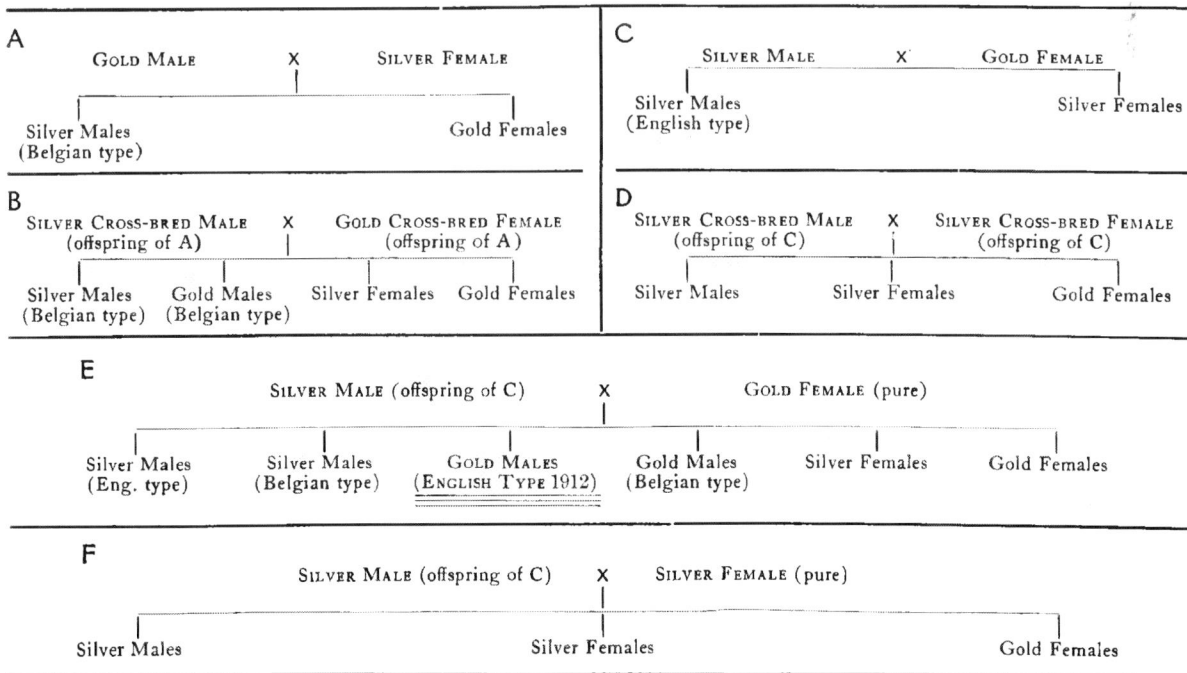

A

GOLD MALE   X   SILVER FEMALE

Silver Males (Belgian type)   Gold Females

C

SILVER MALE   X   GOLD FEMALE

Silver Males (English type)   Silver Females

B

SILVER CROSS-BRED MALE   X   GOLD CROSS-BRED FEMALE
(offspring of A)   (offspring of A)

Silver Males (Belgian type)   Gold Males (Belgian type)   Silver Females   Gold Females

D

SILVER CROSS-BRED MALE   X   SILVER CROSS-BRED FEMALE
(offspring of C)   (offspring of C)

Silver Males   Silver Females   Gold Females

E

SILVER MALE (offspring of C)   X   GOLD FEMALE (pure)

Silver Males (Eng. type)   Silver Males (Belgian type)   GOLD MALES (ENGLISH TYPE 1912)   Gold Males (Belgian type)   Silver Females   Gold Females

F

SILVER MALE (offspring of C)   X   SILVER FEMALE (pure)

Silver Males   Silver Females   Gold Females

Matings of Rev. E. Lewis Jones to Produce English Type Gold Cockerel.

September hatched birds; and, furthermore, their markings were very irregular—as imperfect as was that of the Silvers we knew eight years ago.

We probably shall never be able to state definitely how the first clear-back Silver (winner of Challenge Cup, 1904) was bred. But this production of Dr. Gommers, and my own experiments, indicate one possible way. Possibly, and probably, all the Belgian clear-backed sports (so-called) have originated through crossing with the Frise de la Hollande.

In breeding, as in the science of the derivation of words, the simple and obvious explanation is almost always the wrong one. When a clear-back Silver Campine male was first seen all exclaimed, "Hamburg cross!" The same cry was raised when the clear-back Golden appeared. I knew then this explanation was wrong, for I had failed to produce an English-type male from the Hamburg cross. I said so publicly, but met with incredulity. Many fanciers maintained that they knew how the original Silvers had been bred—even although they could not produce such a male themselves. The challenge I invariably issued was, "Produce an English-type cockerel by Hamburg crossing, and I will believe you." I have now disclosed two methods by which the English-type Golden male can with certainty be produced.

There were certain peculiarities noticed in the offspring of the Gold and Silver Campine crosses. Among others, a tendency to fine barring, like that of the Hamburg. This is perhaps explicable on the assumption that the same laws govern the barring in both breeds. A well-known poultry authority pointed out one of my own Gold pullets to me, and said, "This barring clearly proves a Hamburg cross." The secret of production was a commercial asset to me at that time, so I did not disclose the pedigree of the bird in question. One of the products of mating (c) was unwittingly shown at the Crystal Palace among the Silver cockerels, and he won third prize. This particular bird sired the 1912 winners in Gold Campines, among his offspring being 1st Crystal Palace Gold cockerel, 1st Crystal Palace Gold pullet, and the Gold pullet which created such a sensation at the Royal Lancashire Show (Preston meeting) 1912.

There was a very considerable tendency to red-eye and to sprigs on comb among the progeny. Furthermore, one eye differed in shade from the other. Curiously enough, it was always the same eye which was darker or had more brown pigment than the other. The barring was remarkable for its regularity; in this respect the offspring inherited the perfect barring of the original Silver cock, and not the nondescript markings of the Golden hens. In the majority of the Goldens, the intensity of color was remarkable; but there were a few specimens—male and female—which I can only describe as gold-splashed. We have not yet been able satisfactorily to account for their appearance. Bred inter se, they gave pure Silvers, pure Golds, and gold-splashed birds. I have not been able to pursue this line of breeding this year, but hope to take it up again later on.

————

The following comment on the above article is by John H. Robinson, editor of Farm-Poultry, Boston, and is taken from the June issue, 1914, of that publication:

Mode of Inheritance in the Production of the English-Type Gold Campine Male

Of particular interest in the foregoing valuable article is the observation that "Throughout the whole series of experiments it was immaterial whether cross-bred Silver or pure Silver hens were used; whether cross-bred Gold or pure Gold hens were employed, the male bird was the determining factor." It is not quite clear whether this is intended to apply to Mr. Mattock's experiments only, or to those of Mr. Jones as well, but from the connection it appears to have been the author's intention to apply it to both series of experiments.

The peculiar interest of the statement is that if it correctly interprets the facts, they furnish additional evidence in support of what a correspondent in a recent issue dubbed "Spillman Mendelism." From a first glance at these tables it would appear that the ground color—gold in the one variety, and white in the other variety—of Campines behaved in transmission as it has been claimed by Spillman and his followers that the barring in Barred Rocks and fecundity in hens behave.

When Mr. Mattock mated a Silver male and a Gold female, he got all Silver progeny. In a similar mating Mr. Jones got the same result. When Mr. Jones mated a Gold male and a Silver female, he got Silver males and Gold females. Mr. Mattock, in the second mating in his series, mated a Gold cock to cross-bred Silver-Gold hens from his 1907, with the same result that Mr. Jones got from pure Silver females with a Gold male.

The 1907 and 1908 matings by Mr. Mattock, and the A and C matings of Mr. Jones, gave results which support his statement that the male bird is the determining factor, and which suggest that a Gold hen cannot transmit her ground color to either male or female offspring, while a Silver female may transmit her absence of ground color to her male but not to her female offspring.

When we come to the 1909 mating by Mr. Mattock, however, we find that a mating of a Silver cock with Gold females from a Gold cock with half-Gold females, produced Gold females. It is obvious here that the Gold females transmitted their color to their daughters. Beyond this point, Mr. Mattock's table is apparently incomplete and unsatisfactory. A comparison of his statement of results with Mr. Jones' statement cannot fail to suggest that his statement of results in 1908, and following years, mentions only the material he used, leaving out of consideration what he discarded.

Wherever Mr. Jones has either one or both parents cross-bred he gets a greater variety of results than from a first cross. This is in accordance with common experience and expectation. It is unfortunate that Mr. Mattock's table does not show all the results he (presumably) got.

What strikes anyone with a slight acquaintance with the methods by which new varieties have been produced as singular, is that neither Mr. Mattock nor Mr. Jones made the step after the first mating that most experienced breeders would say was the logical next step. A view which their successful result, when obtained, confirms. Upon what we may call common knowledge of breeding a breeder versed in this knowledge would have assumed at once, after getting the results Mr. Mattock got in 1907 and Mr. Jones in his C mating, that the mating most likely to produce what was sought would be a mating of the cross-bred Silver-Gold male to a Gold female, preferably to his dam.

Type and Color of the Present Day Campine

The Campine Bred for Centuries in Belgium—Some Facts Gathered by the Writer While Visiting European
Countries in 1911—The Introduction of Campines Into England and Subsequent Development—Type
and Color as Found in Best American Specimens, With Some Suggestions for Improvement—Authorities Differ on Color, Making it Imperative That a Color Pattern
be Established at Once, if the Breed is to Progress—The Writer
Believes White Tips on Feathers Should be
Regarded as Defects of Color

By A. O. Schilling

THE story of how the present day English-type Campine came into existence is generally known to breeders on both sides of the Atlantic, but a few remarks upon this subject may not be amiss and will help the reader to a fuller and better understanding of the object of this article.

It is claimed that the old original Campine has existed on the European continent for hundreds of years and was bred by the Belgian peasantry up to the present time as the common barnyard fowl and egg producer. They were referred to by early authorities and writers such as Aldrovandus, during the period A. D. 1600. It is also claimed they existed at the time of Julius Caesar's visit to Belgium; but the facts remain that the breed is native in Belgium and takes its name from the sandy plains or district known as La Campine.

La Campine is a dry, sandy country, and on this soil the breed did not thrive so well and grow so large as the fowls reared on the more moist and loamy soil of the district of Flanders, resulting in the development of two distinct types of the same breed of fowls, one known as the Campine and the other known as the Braekel. Both varieties are clad in identically the same style and color of plumage, the only difference being that the Braekel is larger and heavier than the Campine and varies in type much as do Leghorns and Minorcas.

During the summer of 1911, it was my privilege to study the Campine in England and Belgium and I visited some of the best breeders in both countries. In Belgium I visited the poultry yards of many farmers, and generally found specimens of inferior quality and color, much resembling the duck-wing female color over back and saddle while the breast had some traces of distinct black and white markings. The neck was always silvery white, but as stated above, the back and wings were far from approaching the present-day color of the improved English-type Campines. The Belgian-type male possesses a flowing hackle and saddle of silvery white, while the wing bay is also of same color. In breast these males did not show a tendency to distinct, straight transverse barring, but in type the markings were rather inclined to be crescentic in shape.

It was admitted by several Belgian breeders that specimens of the so-called hen-feathered type male, often appeared among the season's youngsters, but such sports were always discarded as it was believed they lacked

vitality. Thus it remained for the Englishman to conceive the idea of creating a new style of dress for the Campine which seems now so popular with all Campine breeders.

It was in the year 1904 when Mr. J. Wilson, Penrith, England, imported a setting of Campine eggs from Oscar Thomaes, Renaix, Belgium, and among the chicks hatched appeared the first hen feathered Campine male seen in England. The bird was shown that season and seemed to attract much attention and favorable comment. Many other English breeders secured eggs from

The above illustration represents a Silver Campine cockerel exhibited at Kansas City and Chicago shows, December, 1910, by Madame A. F. Van Schelle, of Belgium. This specimen is of the English color type and was the best individual we had seen up to that time. Silver Campines of this style of color were originated by the English in 1904-05, so that he represents five years of breeding along these lines. The feathers accompanying the picture were taken from different sections of his back and saddle and it will be seen they were very clean and distinct even at that time. The neck was very white and free from ticking. His weakest points were breast and wing flights, neither had he the beautiful sickles and barring in tail which the best specimens of today possess. We are not in a position to say whether Madame Van Schelle produced him in Belgium or whether he came from some English breeder, but we are inclined to believe he was of pure Belgium origin, as her entire exhibit was intended to represent the products of the Belgian poultry industry. The beauty of this cockerel's silvery white hackle seems to illustrate our argument and bears out the statement that more consideration should be paid to neck color than the breast. Why not direct our effort to perfecting those sections which are directly visible to the eye at a glance? This would include neck, back, wings, saddle and last and most important of all, a beautiful well furnished tail properly barred with white. The breast will naturally be improved in time by careful breeding, but to sacrifice a beautiful silvery white hackle for the sake of adding more color to upper breast and front of neck does not seem exactly good judgment.—A. O. Schilling.

this mating and from that time on the future of the Campine in England was decided and the improved ideal conceived and created.

The old Belgian Silver-top males were discarded by the English as breeders and gradually by selective mating the breed has developed rapidly toward perfection in color type of plumage. We refer the reader to the illustrations shown on page 64 of four of the finest colored males produced to date. Three of these were shown in 1913-14, while No. 2 is a picture of a cockerel I photographed on my visit to the yards of Rev. E. Lewis Jones of England, in 1911. At that time this specimen was the very choicest I had ever seen and as the Rev. Jones informed me, the best he had produced up to the time of my visit. I am not in a position to state definitely, at this time, whether or not this cockerel is the famous "Silver King," as an eight month old cockerel, for my visit was made to Mr. Jones' yard during the month of September and before the Dairy and Crystal Palace Shows when this cockerel was first shown. "Silver King" was sent to Mr. Kennedy, of Birch Cliff, Ont., and later purchased by Frank Hering, South Bend, Ind., who has been breeding "Silver King" and has produced wonderful results from his matings. The two cockerels No. 1 and No. 4 are by "Silver King" and in our opinion are the finest American bred males shown last season.

Silver Campines were admitted to the American Standard of Perfection in 1893, but dropped again in 1898, owing to lack of interest and the scarcity of the

Messrs. M. R. Jacobus, Aug. D. Arnold, Geo. E. Noeth, J. H. Prudhomme and E. F. Dean. It will be of interest to the reader to observe the vast improvement made in the Campine males by a comparison of the illustration of Madame A. F. Van Schelle's cockerel shown at Chicago, December, 1910, with those shown at New York and Chicago 1913-14. We made photographs and feather studies of Madam Van Schelle's Belgian exhibit at Kansas City and Chicago in 1910, which included various breeds of Bantams, Malines and Campines, and the picture of this cockerel seems very interesting in this connection.

It will be noted that wonderful improvement has been made in development of tail sickles, color of same and that of breast and wing flights. Until the last two seasons males having well furnished, nicely curved

1—The above cockerel was shown at Chicago, 1913, and headed Frank E. Hering's first prize young pen. He embodied many valuable qualities and has a very useful and symmetrical type, in fact, in many ways he may be considered a model, and a fashion plate to follow. His tail barring is wonderful, and in furnishing he is one of the best shown last season.

2—We visited the yards of Rev. E. Lewis Jones, Knighton, England, in October, 1911, and made photographs of some of his best birds. The above cockerel was Rev. Jones' best young male that season and evidently matured into a wonderful cock and proved to be a valuable breeder. Note the excellent clear barring on tail sickles and especially the similarity in combs of cockerels Nos. 1 and 4 to that of No. 2, allowing for the foreshortening caused by the head being turned away from camera. We are inclined to believe this cockerel was "Silver King" as a youngster, the same individual now owned by Frank E. Hering, and which sired cockerels No. 1 and No. 4.

3—This male was the sensational winner in the cock class, 1913, at the Philadelphia Club Show, New York and Palace Shows. He won on color and tail furnishings alone, for he was faulty in shape, being too short and chubby. He was an open barred individual with clear distinct white marking. His black bars were wide and covered with a beautiful green lustre. He had too much color in neck as do all the winners nowadays, but his breast was well marked. No doubt he will make a very valuable breeder for Mr. Rankin, proprietor of Schenley Heights Poultry Yards, Pittsburgh, Pa.

4—We have seen about all the good Campines shown at the large eastern shows thus far, and we do not remember of ever handling a more pleasing cockerel than the one shown above. He was sired by Silver King and is a brother to No. 1 of this group. In size he was just a bit smaller than his brother, but was equally as good in color and tail furnishings and showed more style than his brother. We hope Mr. Hering, South Bend, Ind., will produce more such fine birds. It would help the breed wonderfully if all Campine breeders could own such males to head their breeding yards this season.—A. O. Schilling.

breed in this country. In 1907 M. R. Jacobus, Ridgefield, N. J., made his first importation of the new fashioned English Campine, and to him belongs the credit of the second Campine boom in America. Mr. Jacobus worked hard and patiently in introducing the breed and creating its present day accepted standard. At this time permit me to assure the reader that it is not my intention to antagonize this Standard in any way, but to assist in bringing about a better and fuller understanding of what the ideal Campine should be like and to bring about uniformity in judging at our shows, as well as to assist the amateur in studying the breed thoroughly and carefully.

We publish in connection with this article a full page illustration of a set of male and female feathers, taken from various sections of the body. These feathers represent the very choicest specimens from my own collection together with others sent to me by different breeders of reputation throughout the country. Among the gentlemen who were kind enough to contribute were,

sickles were very rare, in fact did not exist, and in our opinion three of the males shown herewith are the finest of their kind produced to date. Several weeks ago we wrote letters to a number of the most successful breeders and exhibitors for suggestions and opinions on the present accepted Standard. Replies to these letters are published in connection with this article, some of which bring out some very important points for consideration.

We have also prepared a full page illustration representing the ideal male and female (see page 69.) These studies are a combination of the most perfect sections taken from different specimens I have found in the show room up to date, and are drawn in accordance with the present Standard description adopted by the American Campine Club.

We shall not discuss the question of type to a great extent except to give our personal views, which seem to agree in a general way with those of the breeders who have expressed themselves in letters published herewith.

It will be noted that some of these breeders seem to have the Leghorn type in mind as their ideal. While this view is not entirely erroneous, we believe the Campine has and should retain its own individual breed characteristics, in type as it does in color, and in our opinion, to advocate a typical Leghorn shape as the ideal would not be using the best judgment. While the Leghorn type is a very beautiful one in all its harmony of curved sections, still I believe the Campine should be modified in some sections, especially in length of body, fullness of breast and shape of back. The breast should be fuller and more developed, the back should be a trifle longer and curve gradually into juncture of tail and saddle.

In size and weight they should average somewhat heavier than the Leghorn, yet should not approach the Minorca in anyway. The angles of a Minorca are not becoming to a good Campine and should be discouraged. The cockerel illustrated in Fig. 1, page 60, pleases us in many ways, yet he does not entirely fulfill the desired ideal. Cockerel No. 4 possesses many beautiful and desirable qualities and we believe a blending of the two profiles would make nearly an ideal in body shape. No. 3, although a most wonderful colored cock, is too short and cobby for an ideal, while No. 2 is too long and racy, and approaches the Minorca in many ways. This is very apt to be the fault in an immature cockerel at the age at which this bird was photographed.

A well matured female should resemble a good utility Leghorn in shape. She should not show quite so much curve to back and cushion as does the best show Leghorn, but should have enough of this quality to relieve the back line from the straight Minorca shape. She should be rather long in body, well developed in stern, but should not have an excessive low hanging fluff. Campines are sprightly and active and should possess style

The above is a female back feather and illustrates the effect produced by numerous bars on one feather. As a rule female back feathers show from three to four bars and oftentimes only two distinct white bars are seen as illustrated in female back feathers in plate on page 58. To increase the number of bars means to approach the Hamburgh marking and should be discouraged. The white markings on above feather are much too wide according to the present accepted Standard, but even if they were narrow and fine, the possibility of showing off a rich green lustre would not be as good on this type of feather as it would be on a feather with fewer white bars and a broader black ground color.—A. O. Schilling.

and vigor to a large degree. The legs should be set fairly well apart and be moderately long and fine in texture. One of the greatest difficulties to overcome in Campine type has been to establish a low carried tail. This is a fault which I find in most of the pure Belgian birds. The English have improved this defect in a large measure, but we still find many specimens shown in recent years carrying their tails entirely too high.

We venture to say that Americans will improve the type in Campines more rapidly than the English, as low tails are a great hobby with breeders in this country, not only with the Mediterranean breeds, but with our own American varieties. To overcome the production of high tailed specimens our advice is to select as breeders females having plenty of tail coverts and heavy saddles. It will be found that these females produce males with better tail furnishings and full saddles, which will tend to help in a natral way to hold the tail down to a more pleasing angle. Have you ever noticed that the highest tailed males were always those having scant tail furnishings and a lack of flowing saddle feathers at base of tail? Mate your pens to overcome these defects and the Campine will be much improved in type.

A large beefy comb is another eyesore on the average Campine male of today, but we are glad to see considerable improvement has already been made especially in this country. We can recall the time when

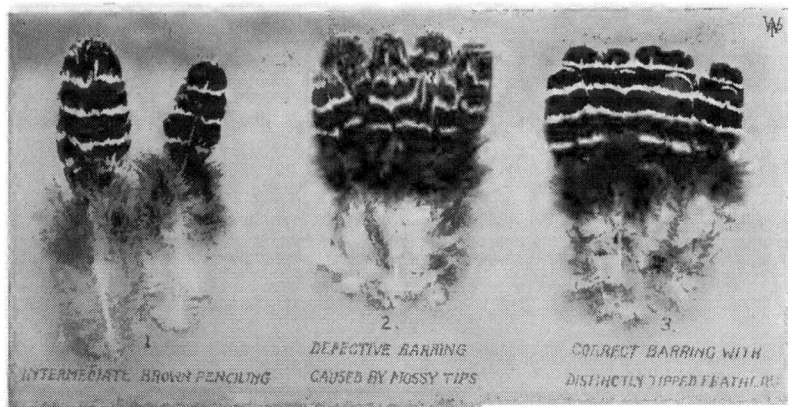

There are three causes for defective marked plumage in the backs and wings of Silver Campines. We have endeavored to illustrate these separately by the photographs of feathers shown above. No. 1 illustrates intermediate barring, which is a common defect among the average flock of Campines, especially those which may have had the old Belgian Braekel color type as their near ancestors. This intermediate barring is like a faint irregular penciling between the two white bars and has a brownish cast of color. Group of feathers No. 2 illustrates mossiness in backs of females. The general tendency is for females to show this defect after they have cast off their original coat of pullet feathers. At present good, clear barred hens of two or three years of age are not numerous. Group No. 3 are select pullet feathers and represent the finest kind of Campine barring as it is produced at the present time. We call attention to the small white tip at end of each feather and note how objectionable this marking is as it lays upon the surface of the black bar on the under-laying feather. The English and American Standards call for this mark on each feather in describing their ideal and we see no reason why this should be so. It is a fact that this characteristic exists in nearly all specimens, more or less, but we hope that breeders will consider this subject carefully and mould their Standard accordingly. If this white tip is not beneficial to the production of clear, distinct barred effect on backs of male or female, why should we describe it as a Standard breed characteristic? We suggest that it be stricken out and eliminated by selection and breeding.—A. O. Schilling.

most Campine males possessed ungainly looking head gear and oftentimes the comb was turned and drooping to one side.

The breeding of color is always a more or less complex problem and it is a difficult matter to advise the beginner just how to mate with assurance of absolute success in his breeding operations. It is generally conceded that a good percentage of show specimens may be produced from one mating, but we have personal knowledge that a few breeders are practicing cockerel and pullet mating to produce their winners. Personally we do not believe this is absolutely necessary if the correct color is established for both male and female. The ideal female should be a specimen possessing nature's own breed marks of a corresponding character and these should be in harmony with that of the male. To follow this law of breeding is to eliminate double mating. Varying ideals are simply the change of fashions created to satisfy the fads of the fancier.

There are cases on record in the history of breeding pure bred poultry where fanciers have created ideals, either in the male or female, which necessitated double mating in order to produce specimens possessing markings and color of the accepted or adopted fashion. We hope that Campine breeders will avoid this condition in the future as their Standard now appears to be perfectly fitting to the breeding of show specimens from single matings.

Authorities Differ On Color

Despite this fact we have recently noticed that some authorities differ in their opinion of what the ideal Campine color should be. On page 16 of the English Campine Club year book for 1914, F. L. Platt writes, "My criticism on the heavy barred male is this: A female with three black bars is not as pretty as one with four black bars. Why not set as the Standard the male that will breed the beautiful females? The male with the wide black bars would never be picked as a pullet breeder. I think that the width of the black bar can be overdone and believe the highest art in breeding will produce a barring that looks refined, not coarse."

In the Poultry Manual, published by Rev. T. W. Sturges, Vice-President of the Poultry Club of England, we find the following:

HINTS ON MATING—The breed is now in the making, so far as the perfection of its marking is concerned. It has so many wants. Among these are: (1) Better combs; (2) white lobes in the cockerel; (3) definite barring on the cock's saddle-hackle—this latter accompanied with a developed tail—and (4) brilliant sheen. When birds approaching the Standard are found there will be little difficulty in mating, since both sexes can be bred from one mating. Until then the best possible must be chosen, taking care not to mate birds together which both contain the same defect.

The Rev. E. L. Jones, one of the most successful breeders, wrote in his Monthly Hints: "The question is how to breed this bird, and it is a question I have been trying to solve for the past four years. First of all see that your breeders have good points, and that their tails are as free as possible from 'greyness' or mossiness. Then select the best marked of your cockerels—dark in color and with rich sheen or lustre. Select from the hens or pullets those which have broad, black bars—too broad for exhibition—and see to it that they are sound in fluff, dark grey in color. Let them, too, be as rich as possible

in sheen. Reject as breeders all that are not sound in eyes, as a wrong eye is very persistent-dominant, as the Mendelists say. Also see that the earlobe of the cockerel is white; it is almost universally so in pullets. In all your breeders always examine the individual feathers and reject any which do not show a white bar (faint it often is) at the end. Rely upon your hens for size, shape and alertness of carriage."

It will be noticed that Mr. Platt suggests breeding for a feather with more black and white bars than the average feather now possesses, while the Rev. E. Lewis Jones advises breeders to select specimens having a wide black bar and states that the females may be those which are too wide for exhibition purposes.

We heartily agree with the Rev. Jones in this respect, for should we aim to produce a specimen with an increased number of bars on the feather it naturally follows that the feather having only a certain amount of surface on which to have these bars, that the bars would have to be crowded together to allow for the additional bars suggested by Mr. Platt. The results would be that the black bar which is now about four times the width of the white bar would be narrowed down, giving only a small narrow space on which to display that beautiful green lustre, one of the chief points of beauty of the Campine. Barred Plymouth Rocks have many bars on the feather, but on such feathers it is almost impossible to show lustre of any amount.

The female back feather shown on plate (page 65) in connection with this article was sent to us by Mr. Jacobus and we believe this is the best specimen feather we have ever seen. It will be noticed that this feather has only three black bars and three white bars not counting the slight white tip. To add another black and another white bar to this feather would be to decrease the width of each, resulting in even finer white bar that we now have, if the comparative ratio of 4 to 1 is to remain. We have selected this wing and back feather as the object of this discussion for the reason that all other feathers vary in length and have more or less bars upon them, depending entirely upon the section of body or back from which they are taken. Wing and back feathers possess the fewest bars and are the shortest feathers upon the bird, therefore, it seems this would be the point of reckoning in determining how many bars a feather should have.

All other feathers from back and saddle which are longer than the shortest back or wing feathers have as many bars upon them as would be possible, depending entirely upon the length of feather and how many times the average width of black and white bars upon the shortest feathers, would go into the length of the longer feathers.

One of the most prevalent defects in color of Silver Campine males is, that the white bar is too indistinct, too fine and narrow. It is not that the black bar is too broad, but that the white bar is not heavy enough to continue across the feather in a clean cut bar without breaking at the quill. Such is the case in most finely barred male saddles, and the sooner we produce an open bar which is clear and distinct, the more beautiful will be the breed.

Mr. Platt states that a female with three black bars is not as pretty as one with four black bars and continues to say, "Why not set as Standard the male that will breed the beautiful females?"

I have just previously pointed out that to increase the

WING-BAR   WING-BOW   LOWER BREAST   UPPER BREAST   WING SECONDARY

LESSER SICKLE

HACKLE

CAPE

4 BACK FEATHERS FROM SHOULDERS TO SADDLE

SILVER CAMPINE MALE FEATHERS

FEMALE MAIN TAIL FEATHER

WING SECONDARY   WING PRIMARY   COVERT   SADDLE   BACK   WING-BOW   BREAST

SILVER CAMPINE FEMALE FEATHERS

In arranging the feathers for the above illustration we endeavored to select only those that closely approach the ideal markings. Some of the above feathers were supplied by leading breeders, while others were taken from our own collection, which embraces feathers selected from winners at leading shows, both in England and America. They are not intended to illustrate the ideal, but from them we may very easily determine how many bars the feathers in each section of the body should have, and also what the type of the barring should be. Standard word descriptions are very helpful and necessary, but nothing can be so complete and accurate as faithful pictures direct from nature. These feathers are a complete set from the most important sections of both male and female, and comply very closely to the present Standard description of Campine color.—A. O. Schilling.

number of bars on the female would naturally tend to produce an increased number of bars on the male as well, also to increase the number of bars would mean to narrow them down in width. At present the natural tendency and most difficult task for Campine breeders is to produce males with a wider, clearer white bar on saddle and back. If Mr. Platt's methods were followed double mating would have to be resorted to in order to produce Standard color males and females, because the finely barred females will produce males of finer barring than the Standard now calls for. It rests with the breeders in general to decide whether or not such advice is to be followed, because as soon as it is, you will establish a double mating Standard.

Personally we can see just as much beauty in a female with two or three bars to the feather as in one with four, and the former with fewer bars is the one which will breed the beautiful males. It should be remembered that we determine the number of bars on the feather by the number of bars on the shortest wing bow and back feathers.

We do not wish to give the reader the impression that we advocate wide, open white barring on the female wing and back, but simply wish to point out the fact that to crowd too many bars upon one feather, would mean to decrease the width of same, making it even more difficult than it now is to produce specimens fit to show.

One of the most neglected sections in the production of Standard bred Campines today is color of neck. We have seen specimens in which the neck hackle showed penciling fully half way up its length, awarded the prize of honor. To our mind one of the distinguishing beauties of the Silver Campine is its pure white neck hackle and we are sorry to see breeders ignoring this quality to such a great extent. The aim has been to produce as much color and barring into the breast as possible, and the desire to perfect this section has been responsible for the great amount of color bred into the silvery white neck hackle. Judges are compelled to make their decisions according to the scale of points in the Standard governing that breed and the fact that the present scale of points allots only five to color of neck and six to that of breast makes it necessary to place the awards accordingly and in harmony with the value of each section, thus enabling the dark neck hackled specimens to win. We believe that this condition should be reversed and six points allotted to neck color and five to color of breast. We would like to see a well marked breast developed, but believe that to retain the beauty of the breed, neck color should receive preference over breast.

There is always room for improvement even in the productions of the best of our efforts. The present Standard was originated by a very capable committee, but despite this fact we need not feel that the height of perfection has been accomplished in Standard making, and to stop where we are and say, "Amen forever" would be poor judgment in our attempt to further the interests and welfare of the breed. E. F. Dean mentions a very important point in his letter and refers to color of main tail feathers of male, which has been omitted from the Standard description. The question is, shall we aim to produce barring in this section or shall the tail remain black?

We believe that an effort should be made to perfect the white markings of main tail feathers, which now already appear in the best specimens. Another reason why the male tail should be barred is that such barring would be in harmony with the corresponding section or tail of female, which all agree should be barred as regularly as possible.

A Standard demanding the tail to be black on the male and barred on the female would in our opinion be contrary to the natural laws of heredity, and would also require double mating to produce these contrasting effects in male and female.

On page 65 will be found an illustration showing three sets of feathers. No. 1, illustrating a very common defect, known as intermediate barring. This blemish to the surface color of the Campine is generally prevalent in back and saddle of the female, also in lesser tail sickles of the male. It is of a brownish hue and should be obliterated by selective breeding. It is a serious defect and should be mentioned as such in connection with a Standard that is supposed to embody our best efforts and be thorough and accurate.

The set of feathers, No. 2 in cut, is intended to illustrate the cause of mossiness on backs of females. It will be noticed that this defect is prevalent upon end of feather, because of the irregularity of the last white bar and a surplus of white tipping at the end of each feather.

This brings up a subject which should receive careful thought and consideration of the breeder. We refer to the white tipping at end of each feather on group No. 3 of same cut. These feathers were selected from the back of a very wonderfully barred pullet and show excellent straight, clear white barring of about the correct relative proportions of black and white. It will be noticed that the white tip at end of feather does not benefit the straight barred effect in the least, in fact is a blemish as it appears on the surface. When the feather ends in the middle of a black bar on the underlying feather, this white tip breaks the regularity of same and we see no reason why breeders should strive to produce it or to incorporate it in a Standard.

The English Standard mentions it and we are also aware that it exists in nearly all strains of Campines, but it is our opinion that to eradicate it, would be a benefit towards perfecting a clear barred breed of chickens. This suggestion may be somewhat premature at this stage of Campine development, but is it not policy and reasonable to study this color problem carefully and thoroughly, and determine the most advisable route to follow in the breeding and mating of Campines towards an ideal which is beautiful?

It may take years to accomplish this, but we feel that we are correct in our conviction regarding this point and it should be considered carefully. If the white tip is not beneficial to allow a clear barred effect to be produced, why not begin now to obliterate such a defect. Breeding fancy poultry to a high standard is a very difficult and complex problem from the color standpoint alone, but this should never become the one great desire and hobby. Shape and vitality are important factors in striving to perfect a breed of fowls which are intended to be useful and ornamental.

Vitality is one of the most important considerations in mating and rearing Campines. Improve this quality by selection and care. Keep the stock healthy and breed from only the most vigorous specimens, and in time the breed will be greatly improved. The following letters were received from a number of prominent Campine breeders and will no doubt be of great interest to the amateur, as they are from men who have been success-

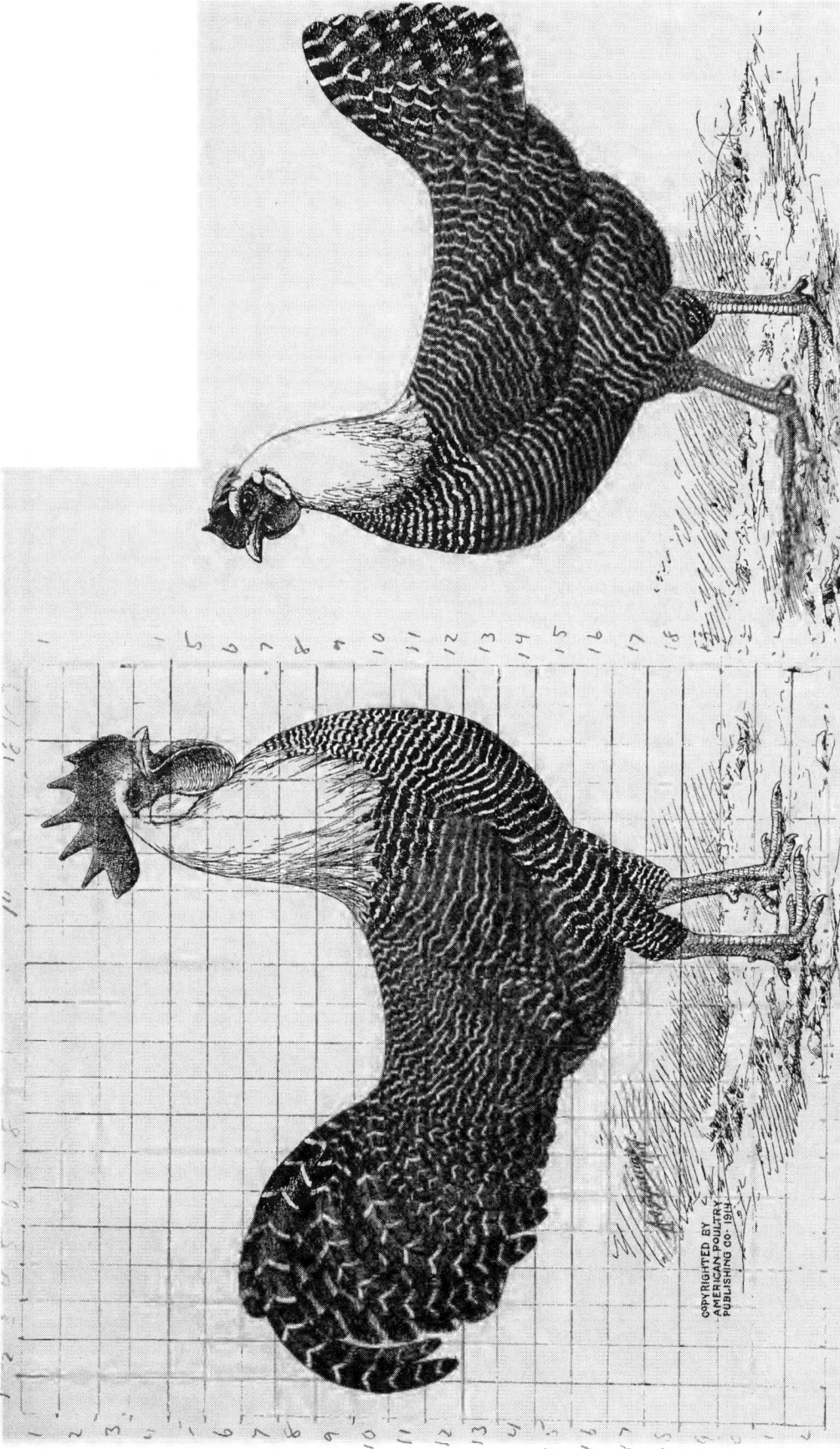

"IDEAL SILVER CAMPINE MALE AND FEMALE"

The above drawings were composed from the studies of the best living specimens found to date, and a careful study of the Campine Standard descriptions as adopted by the American Campine Club, in an attempt to present ideals that would record the progress of the breed, and show the ideal Silver Campine male and female. (Since the above drawing was made, it has been presented for criticism to the Standard Revision Committee of the A. P. A., and while the male was considered nearly ideal, the tail of the female was criticised as too gay and expanded. For ideal female tails see the colored frontispiece).

ful in the show room and are largely responsible for the popularity of the Campine in America:

Markings and Color of Main Tail Feathers Omitted From the Standard

In regard to the shape and color of the tail of males, the Standard calls for sickles well curved and extending well beyond the main tail feathers with lesser sickles and coverts in abundance, with which I am entirely in accord, feeling that the nearer we approach the Leghorn in this section the more Campines will grow in favor. At the recent New York show you will recall an unplaced, yet beautiful little cockerel, from across the pond, which possessed one of those saucy, neat, French mustache appearing tails, he was a little beauty, but here is where the trouble lies, as I have never seen a bird of this type which obtained any size and I doubt if any ever come up to the Standard in weight. There is a very important part which is omitted from the Standard, and that is the markings, or color of the main tail feathers; these I feel should be pure black, devoid of any markings. I should like to hear this section discussed.

Regarding the correct barring on the backs of male and female, we feel that the present Standard is all that could be hoped for, as specimens having barring in this section possess the ratio one to four, are certainly beautiful and possess lustre which could not be obtained if the Standard were changed even so little as to make it one to three. This will be noticed by reference to the samples of feathers herewith enclosed. (The trouble in this section does not seem to be with the Standard, but in the judging). There is another point which we feel should be mentioned here as to the color, i. e., the presence of brown in so many winning birds at our leading shows. While our Standard states that black and white are the colors on a Silver it does not disqualify nor penalize for the presence of brown, it might be said that it does not mention pink, red or even yellow either, but it is our feeling that as brown is so often found in the tails, especially of Silvers, that some mention at least should be made of it. I would not suggest going further than to state that it is a serious defect and should be judged as such.

Taking up the subject of kind or quality of barring of male to be used for breeding exhibition females, I feel, Bro. Schilling, that you are opening a sore, as the leading breeders of this country have been trying to convince the "Poor Unsophisticated Back Lotters" that double matings are absolutely unnecessary. Our experience is that double matings are absolutely essential, in fact we found such to be the case when breeding Leghorns a number of years ago, and the reasons for double mating Campines are very apparent. Our method of mating for exhibition females is not to use a finely barred male with a like barred female, but rather birds of more open barring, not wide open, but of well defined markings on both the male and female and find that the tendency is to tighten in the markings of the progeny. The breast and hackle are also very important factors in mating.—E. F. Dean.

Believes the Campines' Ideal Should Resemble the Leghorn in a General Way

This short communication is in line with my promise made you the other evening.

Personally, I am in favor of a Campine that in type resembles the Leghorn rather than the Minorca, which, I believe, is excellently set forth in the pictures of the two cockerels that you photographed for me.

I am also very strongly in favor of a well feathered tail, with pronounced sickle feathers and a profusion of lesser sickles. I am in favor of lesser sickles, because I think that the green sheen shows to better advantage on these feathers than on any others in the plumage—at least this is so with my strain. I am in favor of the present barring at the ratio of about one to four. I am opposed to very narrow barring.

I am furthermore in favor of having a bird well set up from the ground, with a full breast, and a much smaller comb than we have been able to breed in the Campine.

I also believe in lengthening the body of this bird if necessary, in order to insure plenty of room for the egg laying organs. I think in general the tail is carried at too high an angle, and I would favor an angle as shown in the enclosed pictures.—Frank E. Hering.

Does Not Like the Extremely Narrow Barred Specimens and Believes in Double Mating

My idea of the male Campine is that it should be in time built more after the style of the Leghorn. I would like to see the male with well furnished tail and with long curved sickles clearly barred. I have never liked a high tailed bird, and this has been to my mind a very strong objection to the Campine.

I made some experiments last season in mating, based on the principles that a double mating would produce a better barred specimen than a single mating, but unfortunately the products of these matings were destroyed by rats.

In regard to the barring, I do not like the narrow white bars. It gives the bird too much of a mossy appearance. My idea is that the black bars should be practically four times the width of the white bars on shoulders, wings, back, saddle and tail. The "spidery effect" I do not like. I prefer more black in the bird so that the green sheen which makes the fowl so attractive to the eye, will predominate.—K. M. Turner.

Dislikes Penciled Hackles and Wants More Points Allotted to That Section As Well As Comb

I am in favor of the Standard, only I would prefer to see the combs 6 or 7 points, but points of merit and the tendency has been beefy combs and laced hackles, which I am opposed to, I want to get away from the Barred Rock in neck hackle. Another thing is the flights in the wings. Some run very white and it is hard to get rid of this white—although you see birds photographed and the wings showing correct, when upon examination they have a goodly portion of white in the flight feathers.

Altogether, I think the Standard fair, it was drawn by men who knew the Campines and knew their wants, and while it may be improved upon as the breed progresses, I think in description of type and in outline of barring it fills the bill.

I am in favor of Standard barring, black bar four times as wide as the white bar. I am in favor of long sickle feathers and well furnished low tails, not so low as the Leghorns. I am in favor of saddle feathers, tail coverts and main tail feathers being as long as they can be gotten, that is without being abnormal, but to conform with same parts of Leghorns. I think therein lies the beauty of the bird, and we must have these qualities in the male.

I like the females to be thick and heavy set in the body. I think the body should be heavy. I think a laying breed should be long backed and thick or heavy set at the posterior extremities to give capacity to the egg chamber and to allow space for the formation and growth of heavy, large eggs, for the manufacture of which the Campines have derived fame.—J. H. Prudhomme.

AMERICAN CAMPINE CLUB STANDARD SATISFACTORY

Claims That Rapid Development of Long Sickles Will Tend to Revert Back to Braekel Color and Tinted Eggs

The shape of the Campines is more important than many breeders realize, as one cannot secure the best results from birds which are too broad in body in comparison with the length of the bird.

I have said a lot about the shape of the Campines, but if this shape is neglected it matters little how near perfect one produces his birds in markings to comply with the Standard he will not make a success with the breed, as he will really have handsomely marked feathers on birds that are not truly Campines.

It is also important that breeders strive to have the handsomely marked feathers as called for in our Standard on the bodies of birds of proper shape.

As to the difference of opinion as to the length of the sickles of a Campine male and as to their markings, I personally feel that when we secure, as called for in the Standard, a large full tail, with long, well curved sickles well barred, we will not have injured the Campines in the least as to the egg producing qualities of the breed, but we will then have an exceedingly handsome breed.

We must watch the main sickles and lesser sickles, however, and endeavor to keep them as free as possible from quantities of white at base of feathers or large splashes of white throughout these sickle feathers, as this is an indication of throwing back the Belgian type or of a fresh infusion of Belgian blood.

If we increase the length of the sickle feathers too rapidly and not by degrees the tendency is to throw back to the markings of the Belgian type male as per these white splashes in the sickles.

If one takes a male like this approaching the Belgian type and breeds with females that produce the whitest eggs he will find that a large proportion of the females produced from this mating will not lay as white an egg as their parents, but will have a tendency to produce tinted colored eggs.

I mention this fact to show that the markings called for in our Standard are not only the best for beauty and easiest to reproduce from a single mating, but females bred from a strain that nearest fulfill the requirements of colored markings of the Standard are the ones that produce the whitest eggs.

Where we work for a long tail, however, we must keep close to the Standard and produce a rather long, straight back, slightly sloping to tail and not a curve, as in some of the higher show type Leghorns.

As to the barring of the feathers, both male and female, it is best not to have the white bars too narrow, but whatever the width of the white bars is, the best effect and breeding qualities are secured when the black bar is about four times the width of the white bar.

While the width of the bars is important, it is still more important that each bar be clear cut and well defined and that the white bar does not run into the black bar or vice-versa.

The white bars should be white and the black bars should be greenish black, without any tendency of an intermediate bar.—M. R. Jacobus.

Claims Finely Barred Males Produce Best Show Females

I think the tail of a male Campine should be carried rather low and should be well furnished with long curved sickle. While this is hard to get, yet I think it is what we should have.

As regards barring, I like the white bars rather narrow, but not so fine that they cannot be easily seen at a short distance, for if the white bars are not plainly visible the beauty of plumage does not show at its best. Excepting on breast feathers I think three bars on a male about right. I enclose feathers from a male and female that show off well.

My experience has been that finely barred males produce the best show females.

Also find that the males produce more bars on females than on males.—A. D. Arnold.

We cannot agree with Mr. Arnold in his last statement. We refer the reader to feather chart accompanying this article and you will find that in each relative section the male has more bars on the feather than the female, particularly in wing bow, wing bar, back and saddle. Male's feathers are longer and naturally have room for more bars.

How to Organize and Conduct a Specialty Club

The Reason Why the American Campine Club Was Organized—How a Permanent Organization Was Effected—Naming the Club—The Work of Securing Memberships—How to Handle a Specialty Club.

By M. R. Jacobus, Secretary of the American Campine Club, Ridgefield, New Jersey

ALTHOUGH I am a member of a number of clubs and societies not only those devoted to poultry, but also in other lines, it has not been my good fortune to be directly interested in the formation of more than one, this one being the American Campine Club. So in answer to the title of this article, "How to Organize and Conduct a Club," I will explain what lead up to the formation of the American Campine Club, as well as describing how the club was organized and managed.

Being a breeder of the Campines for some time previous to the formation of the American Campine Club, and as I was very anxious to have only the highest type of Campines introduced into America, I felt the need of a good live American club devoted to the Campine breed. At that time not having had any experience in the formation of clubs as explained above, I personally hesitated in starting this work, hoping to find some experienced party to handle it. The longer time I waited the more necessary it became to have a club that would not only use the combined efforts of its members to secure the adoption of a Standard calling for the type of Campines best fitted for America and to encourage the breeding of such, but which club would, through the co-operation of its members, also use its best efforts to discourage the breeding of unprofitable types.

This was without doubt more important with the Campines than with any other breed ever introduced into America, for at that time there were being imported into our country birds of many types, most of which were not suited for best results in our country, although big money was being sent abroad for them in the purchase price, in addition to the importing charges. Realizing that such would injure and soon ruin the breed if a club was not organized to adopt a proper type, I finally brought this matter to the attention of Mr. Frank L. Platt, associate editor of the Reliable Poultry Journal, one evening in March, 1911, in the library room of my home. Mr. Platt, like myself, realizing the necessity of a Campine club, gladly aided in advice. After talking over the good work that such a club could accomplish and carefully considering the formation of a club, we decided that evening that a temporary organization should be formed having a chairman pro tem and secretary pro tem. I do not now recall which of us first suggested the name of Mr. George Urban, Jr., of Buffalo, N. Y., but we both were of the opinion that if Mr. Urban could be induced to act as temporary chairman of a Campine club that he would be the correct man to head such a club, he being not only interested in the breed the club was to represent, but he was a thorough fancier in every way and thoroughly qualified to aid in the formation of such a club.

When I asked Mr. Platt if he could suggest some one to act as secretary pro tem, he, to my surprise, suggested that I should act. When I explained that I had not any experience along this line he suggested that as I was deeply interested in the welfare of the breed that it was my duty to act. Knowing the necessity of an American club and realizing the time was fully ripe for the formation of such a club, I then decided to act as secretary pro tem until a permanent organization could be effected.

That same evening we decided to get in touch with Mr. Urban and if possible to secure his good offices to help in the organization of such a club. Shortly after this I went to Buffalo and met with Mr. Urban and several others interested in the welfare of the Campines. Mr. Urban then agreed to act as chairman and I to continue as secretary pro tem.

The success or failure of the club and possibly the breed depended largely upon what was done at this meeting.

At this Buffalo meeting in the selection of a name it was decided that the club be called "The American Campine Club." The selection of this name may now appear very simple; at that time it was not. I personally consider that here is where the success or failure of the club and breed hung in the balance.

Previous to the Buffalo meeting many Brackel were being sold as Campines and some were confusing the Braekel with the Campines, and there was a desire on the part of some to have the Campines called the Brackel-Campines.

If the name Brackel had been added to the club's name many Braekel would have been imported as Campines and this confusion would have, of course, injured the breed. I mention these facts to show that in the beginning or at the formation of a club it is very important to select the most suitable name, in short, the name must stand for what the club is to represent.

After the selection of a name for the club an organization committee was selected whose duties were to arrange for and perfect a permanent organization.

After the meeting at Buffalo there remained much work to be done before a permanent organization could be effected.

To secure the support of a large number of Campine breeders and assure a good attendance of Campine breeders at a general meeting, it was decided to call such a meeting, to be held at Madison Square Garden Poultry Show, in December, 1911, inviting all breeders of Campines to attend and lend this aid in the formation of a permanent organization.

Knowing my inexperience in the work connected with the formation of a club, I realized that it would be necessary for me if I was to be of any service to the club in its work to give every little detail careful attention.

At this point in the formation of the club many personal letters were written to breeders and others interested in the breed, inviting them to attend the Madison Square Garden meeting and join the club, these personal letters being in addition to printed letters, sent to individuals and the press.

I also sent out requests and blanks to each breeder I knew of or could get in touch with, asking them to send in the names of all parties they knew to be interested in the breed so that I could send them an invitation to attend the New York meeting, as well as application blanks to join the club. This brought in the names of other Campine breeders to whom invitations were sent, asking them to attend the New York meeting and join the club.

This was the means of securing a nice number of applications for membership to the club, which applications were acted upon at the Madison Square Garden meeting. To each person making application for membership to the club was sent a personal letter thanking him for his application. With this letter were also sent more application blanks for distribution among other interested persons.

The practice of writing personal letters of thanks to all who apply for membership and of sending out other application blanks to new members, I still continue at the present day. The letters I find are appreciated and help to make each member feel that he is a part of the club.

Several parties interested in the Campines were very generous in donating funds towards a nice line of special prizes to be offered at the Madison Square Garden Show, where the permanent organization was to be formed. A list of these special prizes was sent to all breeders of Campines that I, as secretary pro tem, could get in touch with. In addition, this list of special prizes and notices of meeting, etc., were sent to at least 100 papers interested in poultry work. Many of these publications kindly published these notices.

Through the personal letters and notices sent out to breeders and the printed notices in the poultry press much interest was aroused in the exhibit of Campines and the meeting for the formation of a permanent organization, with the result that when the meeting was called to order ninety-six had already made application to join the club and before the day was over one hundred members had been enrolled.

The enthusiasm shown in the meeting by active fanciers was the means of not only forming upon a good basis a permanent organization, but assured the election of a full board of active officers and executive board.

After the formation of this permanent organization with elected officers and executive board the club was in a position to carry on the work in a proper business-like manner, which was impossible when it was only a temporary organization represented by temporary officers. The officers and executive board elected when the permanent organization was formed being all active and willing to work for the upbuilding of the club meant the success of the permanent organization.

For the success of any club it is very important to have an active executive board, each member of which will reply without delay to all letters from the secretary, asking for a vote or advice of the board. A few inactive members on such a board will handicap the progress of any club.

The secretary must have and retain the confidence of the club's members, so if he is for any reason unable to receive sufficient replies to any of his letters to the executive board he can proceed with pressing matters to the best of his judgment. A secretary without the confidence of the club's members would be of little use to any club, as this would be a severe handicap in the handling of the club's work.

Since the formation of the permanent organization when I was elected secretary, I have handled the secretary's work very much along the lines they were handled during the interval when I was acting as secretary pro tem and using my efforts to secure a large number of applications for membership to the club and to secure a successful meeting for the formation of a per-

manent organization. This includes the writing of many personal letters to Campine breeders who should become members of the club, and sending out large numbers of application blanks in what might almost be called an endless chain system.

When a new member receives his membership card as explained before in this article, he receives a letter thanking him in behalf of the club for his application. Along with this letter is sent a number of application blanks for distribution among interested parties, in addition to this at frequent intervals numbers of application blanks are sent to each club member with the request that they distribute them among interested parties.

The system of offering special ribbons as is done in other clubs, has of course been followed by the American Campine Club, however when the club was young and not in a position to offer specials at the larger part of the shows throughout the country, I endeavored as secretary to distribute the ribbons the club did offer as widely as possible. As these ribbons were for competition only to members of the club or to those who made application previous to the date of the show at which the ribbons were offered, this was the means of not only bringing in new members to the club, but it brought in closer fellowship the members in the section of the country at which they were offered.

Since explaining why and how the club was organized and since managed I will sum up briefly what I consider very important for the successful formation and handling of a club.

1st. A suitable name. That is, the name selected should represent as much as possible what the club stands for.

2nd. Suitable officers. Officers should be selected who are interested in the work and success of the club and such as have and can retain the full confidence of the club's members.

3rd. Workers. Officers must be composed not only of interested parties, but of such members as have the time and are willing to attend to every little detail of the work of the office they are elected to fill.

4th. Letter writing. For a club to advance and be of any service to its members, the secretary must be one willing to give a large amount of time to personal letter writing, to individual parties, in addition to the large number of notices necessary to be continually sent out to members, the press and other interested parties.

5th. Advertising. To gain any ground it is absolutely necessary to advertise thoroughly. Not only advertise through the correct mediums, but also a proper method and system must be pursued and continued. The above, of course, includes getting in and keeping in touch with all parties known to be interested in the work.

6th. Interest and enthusiasm. For the successful growth of a club it is very important to keep up the interest and enthusiasm in the club's work. Without this the club will be at a standstill or lose ground.

7th. Each member a part of the club. Each member must be made to fully realize that he is a part of the club and that his help is not only desired but also necessary for the most successful work and growth of the club.

8th. Results. The work of the club must be such that results are accomplished, not only results that can be seen by club members, but results that will be observed by those who are not members of the club, whether they are directly interested or not in the line of work which the club represents.

The Organization of the American Campine Club

Note:—Following is the report of the secretary which was mailed to the members of the American Campine Club, after the organization of the club had been perfected, and the first meeting held at Madison Square Garden, during the poultry show, December, 1911:

The American Campine Club
Office of the Secretary

Member American Campine Club:—

Ridgefield, N. J., June 1st, 1912.

Dear Member: It having been decided that the American Campine Club this year was hardly in a position to issue a Year Book, I am sending each member this circular letter giving a small report of the meeting of the club, held at Madison Square Garden, New York, Show, December 21st, 1911, when a permanent organization was formed.

I am not only sending a list of the members received at the New York meeting, but also a list of the members whose applications have been received since the New York meeting, and passed by the executive board.

The New York meeting was called to order by Mr. Geo. Urban, Jr., chairman protem.

M. R. Jacobus, secretary protem, read the minutes of the meeting held at Buffalo, N. Y., May 17th, 1911, when a temporary organization was formed. After approval of the minutes of the Buffalo meeting, the secretary protem reported that he had 96 applications for membership to the club. Upon roll call 24 of these answered to their names.

Motion was made and unanimously carried that a permanent organization be formed and upon further motion the following applicants were received as members to the club. (Here follows a long list of names omitted here).

The following were appointed as officers:

Mr. Geo. Urban, Jr.—President.

Mr. F. Harrison—Vice-President.

Mr. M. R. Jacobus—Secretary-Treasurer.

Mr. F. L. Platt—Vice-President.

Rev. E. Lewis Jones, England; Madam A. F. Van Schelle, Belgium; J. Fred N. Kennedy, Canada, Honorary Vice-Presidents.

Mr. J. M. Foster, Geo. E. Noeth, and Dr. Thos. J. Clemens were appointed on the executive board with the president and secretary.

Motion was made and carried that the American breeders use as a guide the Standard of the Campine Club of Great Britain this season and that the executive board draw up a Standard to be presented at the next meeting of the club. The executive board was also instructed in drawing up their Standard to endeavor to procure an International Standard.

(Signed) M. R. JACOBUS, Secretary.

CAMPINE STANDARD
America's First Campine Standard

Note:—This Standard is copyrighted by the American Campine Club and is reprinted here for its historical value. This Standard was submitted to the members of the American Campine Club and at the annual meeting of the club, Madison Square Garden, December, 1912, a committee was appointed to revise and perfect this Standard, and the committee met in Buffalo, January, 1913, and the Standard that this committee drew up was submitted to the club and accepted by a mail vote, March 17th, 1913.
The club, through its secretary, Mr. Jacobus, made application for the admission of the Silver and Golden Campines to the American Standard of Perfection. This was in the spring of 1914. The question of standard came before the Standard Revision Committee of the A. P. A. at its meeting in Chicago, May 11-12, 1914, and the Campine Standard was referred back to the writer for such changes as would make it conform to the general character of the A. P. A. Standard.
The application of the Campines to the Standard was voted on by the general convention of the A. P. A. at the annual meeting, which was held in Chicago, August 10-14, 1914, and the Campine became a Standard breed recognized in two varieties, Silver and Golden. For the new and complete Campine Standards see the American Standard of Perfection.—Ed.

Proposed Standard Offered for Adoption By American Campine Club

Campine Standard

Copyright 1912 By American Campine Club
All rights reserved
Ridgefield, N. J., Dec. 4th, 1912.

To the Members of the American Campine Club:—

Gentlemen: After conferring with Mr. Frank L. Platt, Vice-President of the American Campine Club, who has carefully studied the Campines in England and Belgium, as well as in America, we decided that the following proposed Campine Standard will best fill the requirements for America.

To protect this Standard for the exclusive use of the American Campine Club I have had it copyrighted in the club's name. Kindly study this Standard carefully and be ready to report at the meeting of the club, to be held at Madison Square Garden, January 2nd, 1913, at 2:30 P. M., at which time a vote will be taken on the adoption of a Standard.

Very respectfully,

M. R. JACOBUS, Secretary.

Campines—Silver and Golden
Scale of Points

Symmetry	4
Size	4
Condition	4
Head—Shape 2, Color 2	4
Beak—Shape 2, Color 2	4
Comb	10
Eyes—Size 3, Color 5	8
Wattles and Ear-lobes—Shape 5, Color 5	10
Neck—Shape 3, Color 4	7
Back—Shape 4, Color 4	8
Tail—Shape 6, Color 4	10
Wings—Shape 3, Color 4	7
Breast—Shape 4, Color 5	9
Body and Fluff—Shape 3, Color 2	5
Legs and Toes—Shape 4, Color 2	6
	100

FIRST PRIZE SILVER CAMPINE COCKEREL & PULLET & FIRST PRIZE GOLDEN CAMPINE COCKEREL & PULLET, GRAND CENTRAL PALACE NEW YORK DEC. 1912. MANHATTAN FARMS, Geo. E. NOETH Proprietor, BRIGHTON N. Y.

At the New York and Boston Shows of 1912-13, we found large classes full of the best quality ever shown in this country and equal to the best we have seen in England or Belgium. We were surprised with the quality in the Goldens especially, as we found males having type and color, equal to many of our best Silvers. It is remarkable to note the general uniform type in both Golden and Silver males and females shown above. Manhattan Farms have surely proven themselves producers of the champions in Campines of this country—A. O. Schilling.

Standard Weights

Cock ....6 lbs.
Cockerel .... .5 lbs.
Hen ....4 lbs.
Pullet ....3 lbs. *

* This weight was later increased to 3½ lbs.

Disqualifications

All general disqualifications apply to the Campines. See American Standard of Perfection, pages 32 and 33; edition of 1910.

Breed Disqualifications

Red covering more than one-half of the ear-lobes. Red or bay eyes. White in face. Legs other than leaden blue. Two or more white saddle hangers on the back of a Silver Campine male. Two or more reddish bay saddle hangers on the back of a Golden Campine male. Black and white bars of equal width in the back plumage of a Silver Campine. Black and reddish bay bars of equal width in the back plumage of a Golden Campine.

Shape of Male

Head: Moderate in length and fairly deep.

Beak: Moderate length.

Comb: Single. Medium size, straight and upright, following the shape of the skull with the blade proceeding slightly under horizontal; five distinct points; serrations deep and points pencil pointed.

Eyes: Large, bright and prominent.

Wattles and Ear-lobes. Wattles: A little longer than medium. Well rounded, smooth in texture. **Ear-lobes:** A broadened almond shape, smooth, of moderate size, fitting closely to head.

Neck: Medium length, nicely arched, and well furnished with hackle.

Back: Rather long, slightly sloping to tail, not too broad at shoulders and carrying this width the entire length. Back feathers over hips, the longer the better.

Tail: Well expanded, main feathers carried 45 degrees above the horizontal; sickles well curved and extending beyond main tail feathers; lesser sickles and coverts, the more abundant the better.

Wings: Large, well folded and tucked up.

Breast: Deep, well rounded and carried well forward.

Body and Fluff: Body moderate length and fairly deep. Not a sharp appearing body from behind. Fluff neat.

Legs and Toes: Thighs and shanks rather long and slender. Shanks round and not feathered. Scales neat and finely laid on. Toes, four on each foot, rather long, slender and straight.

Shape of Female

Head: Moderate in length, fairly deep, well rounded.

Beak: Moderate length.

Comb: Single, medium size, five distinct points, deeply serrated, the first point upright and balance of comb falling gracefully to one side, fine in texture.

Eyes: Large, bright and prominent.

Wattles and Ear-lobes. Wattles: Moderate size, well rounded, fine texture. **Ear-lobes:** Oval in shape, smooth, thin, fitting closely to the head.

Neck: Medium length, slender, slightly arched.

Back: Rather long, declining slightly to tail, not too broad at shoulders, somewhat rounded across cape.

Tail: Long, full, well spread, carried at an angle of forty degrees above the horizontal.

Wings: Large, well folded and tucked up.

Breast: Deep, well rounded and carried well forward.

Body and Fluff. Body: Moderate length, fairly deep. Not a sharp appearing body from behind. **Fluff:** Neat.

Legs and Toes: Thighs and shanks rather long and slender. Shanks round and not feathered. Scales neat and finely laid on. Toes, four on each foot, rather long, slender and straight.

Silver Campines
Color of Male and Female

Head: Plumage white.

Beak: Horn.

Comb: Red. Some blue at base of comb in females permissible.

Eyes: Black.

Face: Red.

Wattles and Ear-lobes. Wattles: Red. **Ear-lobes:** White.

Neck: Hackle surface white. Undercolor slate.

Plumage: Every feather on the bird's body, with the exception of those of the neck hackle, should be barred in a transverse direction. These bars should be as clear as possible, with well defined edges; they should run across the feathers so as to form as near as possible rings round the body. The barrings in the feathers of the shoulders, saddle hackle and tail may run in a more or less V-shaped direction. The bars in all cases should be clear, well defined and with clear-cut edges. The black bars should be nearly as possible three times the width of the white bars. The white must be clear and distinct; the black should be greenish black, the more lustre the better.

Shanks and Toes: Leaden blue.

Golden Campines
Color of Male and Female

The same standard as required in the Silvers, except substitute "reddish bay" for "white" in the plumage color.

The English Campine Standard
From "The Poultry Club." Standards, England

Campines (Non-Sitters)—General Characteristics
Cock

Head—Skull: Moderately long and deep and inclined to width. **Beak:** Rather short. **Eyes:** Prominent. **Comb:** Single, of medium size, upright, evenly serrated, free from excrescences, the back carried well out but clear of the neck. **Face:** Smooth. **Ear-lobes:** Of medium size, inclined to almond shape and free from wrinkles. **Wattles:** Fairly long in proportion to the comb and of fine texture.

Neck—Of medium length and well furnished with hackle.

Body—Broad, narrowing to the tail, close and compact, rather long back, full and round breast, large and neatly tucked wings.

Tail—Of good length, carried well out from the body and with broad and plentiful sickles and secondaries.

Legs and Feet—Legs: Of medium length and

shanks free of feathers. Toes: Four on each foot, slender and well spread.

Carriage: Alert and graceful.
Weight: 7 lbs.

Hen

With the exception of the comb, which falls over one side of the face, the general characteristics are similar to those of the cock, allowing for the natural sexual differences.

Weight: 5 lbs.

Color

Beak: Horn. Eyes: Iris, dark brown; pupil, black. Comb, face and wattles: Bright red. Ear-lobes: White. Legs and feet: Leaden blue. Toe nails: Horn.

The Silver

Plumage—Head and neck-hackle: Pure white. Remainder of plumage: Ground color pure white, and barring pure black with rich beetle-green sheen, every feather being barred in a transverse direction with the end white, the bars clear and with well defined edges, running across the feather so as to form, as near as possible, rings around the body, and three times the width of the ground (white) color. On the breast and underparts of the body the barrings should be straight or sightly curved, but on the back, the shoulders, the saddle hackle and the tail of a V-shaped pattern. The cock should be furnished with properly developed saddle hackles.

The Gold

Plumage—Head and neck-hackle: Rich gold, and not washed out yellow. Remainder of plumage: Ground color rich gold and barring pure black with rich beetle-green sheen and markings as in the Silver.

Scale of Points

Markings	30
Color: Neck hackle 12, sheen 10	22
Size	10
Condition	10
Tail (development and carriage)	8
Comb	5
Eyes	5
Lobes	5
Legs and feet	5
	100

Serious defects: Even barring; penciled ground color; sprigs on comb; legs other than leaden blue; white in face; red eyes; feather or fluff on shanks.

The Belgian Campine Standard

Translated by Madame A. F. Van Schelle, Belgium

General Appearance: Medium sized fowl, "svelte" (graceful), elegant, lively. Single combed, distinguished by its plumage, barred with black on a foundation either white or gold, with neck hackle either white or gold. Eye, black; ear-lobe, white; legs, blue.

Cock: Single combed, erect, having five or six regular teeth with posterior lobe larger, and sloping away a little from the nape of the neck. Advancing in front a little over the beak. Texture, rather fine. Not too developed combs preferred.

Beak: Blue, sometimes clear horn color at extremity.

Eye: Vetch (chick pea), that is to say, very dark—appearing black. Eyelid, often blackish.

Face: Red, covered with little feathers.

Ear-lobes: Almond-shaped, bluish white, or mother-of-pearl white, smooth if possible, often a little wrinkled.

Wattles: Not too long, five to six centimetres, drooping, same texture as the comb.

Head: Medium size, slightly flattened.

Neck: Well proportioned, adorned with abundant hackle, reaching to middle of the back. Neck slightly arched.

Breast: Quite large and very fleshy. Sternum rather long.

Wings: Long, well developed, held very tightly against body and carried rather low in a haughty manner.

Back and Loins: Well proportioned to the general harmony of the body, neither too long nor too short.

Tail: Well developed, carried semi-horizontally.

Thighs: Rather short, hidden in the downy feathers of the abdomen, bones fine.

Shanks: Medium length, slender, very smooth, light blue slate color. Toes: Four; slender, medium length.

Nails: Bone-white, slightly gray at extremity.

Carriage: Proud, haughty, easy gait.

Flesh: Exceedingly fine and succulent.

Weight: Unlimited for adult bird.

Hen

The same characteristics as those of the cock, except that the comb droops during egg laying period, often streaked with blue pigment. The ideal comb should stand up straight at the base, then fold over on one side of the head.

Wattles and Ear-lobes: Are less developed. Eyelid, often darker than in cock; head more slender. Weight, unlimited. Very abundant egg-layer; eggs white-shelled. Non-sitting. Sometimes hens become broody as an exception and bring their brood up well.

Silver Cock

The plumage in general, is white with black bars, except the hackle. Neck hackle, entirely white, but if the feathers are examined, generally a little gray follows the feather lengthwise. The second year, cocks often have a little gray in the lower part of (base of) neck hackle. Feathers between the shoulders, well barred with white on a black ground color.

Epaulettes: Black feathers with all the visible part silver-white, sometimes there is a little point at the extremity.

Wing Flights: Black, more or less marked with white on the exterior part.

Hen: Idem.

Cock

Flight Coverts: As much as possible marked transversely, the white bar more or less broad, alternating with black bars. Green metallic sheen.

Secondaries: Idem. Black bars, green sheen, very intense.

Wing Coverts: Well barred, not so wide. Between the shoulders, little feathers, more or less barred.

Feathers of Loin: Black, the part showing, white. (Important).

Breast: Under the beak, feathers have one or two rather broad white bars. A little lower down, the number of white bars increases, but they are narrower. All of the breast, the feathers of the down, of the thigh, should be well barred.

Tail: Main tail feathers, black as they can be, bordered with gray or white.

The Sickles: Black or bordered with gray or white. The lesser sickles black or slightly laced. The small sickles, if possible, well barred.

Hen

Flight Coverts: Regularly barred.
Secondaries: Idem.
Wing Coverts: Idem.
Feathers of Loin: The white bar on the back and loins become very narrow.
Breast: Most clearly and regularly barred, a little lighter under the beak.
Tail: Black-grayish.

The Sickles: The two large sickles barred if possible. The lesser sickles barred.

Gold Campines

Same standard as for the Silver, substituting the word "Gold" in place of "White." The ground color gold, as intense as possible, not a washed-out yellow.

Serious Defects—(Disqualifications)

1. Squirrel or wry tail.
2. Feathers on the leg, or color other than blue.
3. More than four toes.
4. Comb other than single, sprigs or over-developed comb.
5. Red eye (in young fowls).
6. White in the face.
7. Equal width bars.
8. Barred wing-bow, or saddle feathers barred.

Study of Campine Feathers

By Rev. J. N. Wynne Williams B. A. England

EVEN among Campine breeders there seems a lack of knowledge as to what the requirements of a Campine are. Judging quite recently at a show, where there was a Campine class, I was accosted afterwards by a young lady, who, with every mark of disappointment in face and tone, yet enquired gently why her birds had not won. I went into particulars with her, and I am satisfied she went away with a much fuller knowledge of Campines than she had before the judging.

Therefore, a word to novices upon essentials. There are things very desirable and those absolutely anathema about Campine feathers. A poor bird has no sheen whatever, a dead, sooty black, and it hardly matters how well marked it may be if the feathers have no lustre, the bird is not much good as a show bird. This class of bird is very liable to have fawn markings, and a good deal of pepper and salt, in the sickles particularly. The sheen must be a brilliant beetle green, and ought to show itself all over the bird. That is one point.

Another is clarity of ground color. Whether gold or silver, it must be clear. Really, the white and the gold are the ground color; but with a sort of unaccountableness that I cannot quite make out, the usual mode of talking about the markings of Campines has, I am informed, been reversed by the committee of the Campine Club, and the black is the ground, and the white or gold the bars. Strange! Whatever can have brought about the reversal of that which has been the proper way ever since barring was barring in the poultry fancy? Personally, I stick to the old way! No pepper and salt in the ground color anywhere!

The black must be very sharply and very broadly

cut, indeed. It does not in all feathers run quite transversely across the web of the feather. In the saddle hackles, of which I here give an illustration, it will be seen that in some feathers there is a distinct inclination for the marking to arch across the web, whereas towards the tip of the feather the white runs more in what would be termed mackerel marking.

Each of these feathers here sketched was produced in the reality. They are all drawn from "life" and are not a fabrication of an ideal which has never yet been produced. We want to see this hackling brought more and more to perfection. For a while it ought to be bred for specially. I think a few seasons would produce it. The trio of feathers sketched shows the very broad barring insisted on for Campines by the Standard. I would specially draw the attention to the tips, which are black and not gray. That fatal grayness at the tip destroys all symmetry of marking. It does not help to form the beautiful rings at all, but, on the contrary, confuses them dreadfully.—Reprinted from "Poultry," London, Eng.

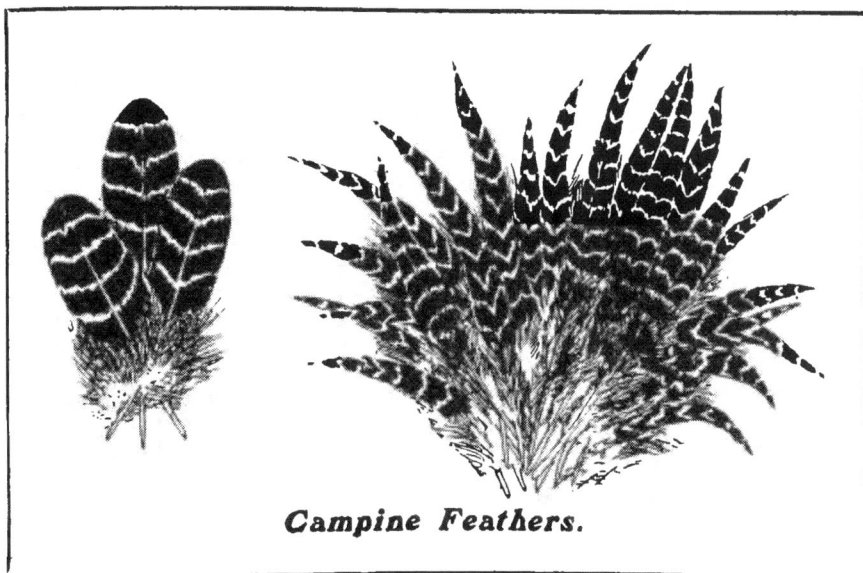

Campine Feathers.

What Constitutes an Ideal Campine

An Explanatory Standard for Breeders and Judges—The Ideal Bird, Section by Section, is Described, and the Faults Pointed Out—How to Measure the True Value of an Exhibition Campine.

By F. L. Platt

COMB: There was some question whether the Campine comb should have wedge shaped spikes, or round, pencil pointed spikes, and the latter was decided upon as Standard. The comb should be about the size of a Leghorn's comb, but the blade should have a tendency to follow the neck. The blade should not rest on the back of the head and neck as in the Minorca, being intermediate between the Leghorn and Minorca in this respect. The heavier blade gives the Campine comb a slightly heavier appearance than the Standard Leghorn comb. In the female, the comb should rise to the first point and then fall gracefully to one side. Some blue at the base of the female comb is neither a defect nor does it indicate a debilitated condition. It is a characteristic of the Braekel. Combs on Campines have been improved remarkably in the years 1911-14.

Eyes: The eye should be large and bright. The pupil of the eye should be black and the iris nearly so. "Black" would describe the color of the eye were it not that in a close study, a purely and positively black eye is not found in our domestic chickens. In the Silver Campines a red eye is a serious defect and such a specimen should not be bred or a first prize hung on it. If there is only one bird in the class, withhold the first and award a second prize. In a large show like New York, only a few red eyed Silvers will be seen and these should be passed without a ribbon. In the Golden, the situation is different. Blackish eyes are rarely seen, especially in the males, and a dark eye in a Golden cockerel will invariably come red as the bird ages into the cock stage. Red eyes in this variety therefore, should not be severely penalized either by the breeder or judge.

FIRST PRIZE COCKEREL, BOSTON, JAN. 1912. FIRST PRIZE PLLT, MADISON SQUARE GARDEN, DEC. 1911
SPECIAL, BEST FEMALE, SPECIAL BEST COLORED FEMALE, MADISON SQUARE GARDEN DEC. 1911
M·R·JACOBUS, RIDGEFIELD, N·J·

Those who attend the New York and Boston Shows have become familiar with the Campines belonging to M. R. Jacobus, Ridgefield, N. J. Mr. Jacobus has won a number of important first prizes on the large, white eggs of his Campines in the regular classes at Boston. The Campine egg is quite an equal oval, large at both ends and it has a smooth surface with a good thick shell that insures safe transportation. It has been celebrated for a half century or more in Belgium. Mr. Jacobus has done more than any other man in America to make known the good qualities of the Campine and to establish its record as a profitable egg hen. He has also won a large share of first prizes at the Boston and New York Shows. The pullet shown above that won first and special at Madison Square Garden, Dec., 1911, is very close to Mr. Jacobus' Ideal. The sturdy cockerel as well as the pullet exhibits the long, level body that Campine breeders are selecting as the most valuable.

Wattles and Ear-lobes: The ideal wattle does not hang low nor is it folded. The ear-lobe should also be of medium size and smooth. Red is a defect found in the lobes, especially of males. Where red covers more than one-half of the lobe the bird should not be placed. A lobe that is white is ideal and one inclined to a bluish white is preferable to one inclined to a yellowish white. Indeed, a slight tint of blue is not considered a defect in the English shows.

Neck: A good furnish of hackle is desired. There is a certain length and arch that comes naturally with an active breed such as the Campine, so a description of the shape of the neck would be technical and not essential. The neck should be white in both sexes of Silvers and golden bay in the Goldens. The neck is the only section of the bird that is not barred, and as it is a distinctive section for that reason, setting off the bird by way of contrast, it is desirable that there should be practically no barring in the hackle or neck feathers. It is quite unusual however, to find sound breast barring and sound back barring on a bird with a pure colored hackle. Plenty of cheap birds have white or golden hackles—the farm flocks in Belgium have this section in perfection. Only studious, persistent breeding produced the back and throat barring and therefore when these two sections are found good, the judge or breeder must bear a bit with nature and not criticise the bird too severely for carrying some of the color into its lower hackle plumage. While the pure colored hackle is beautiful and desirable, it should not be secured at the loss of back and breast feather properties and judges should balance these qualities before awarding their color specials.

Back: There has been some thought as to whether the back should concave as in the Leghorn or be nearly straight to tail. Because of the utility value of the longer, straighter back this type has become standard in judging females, both at the leading shows in America and in England. To accord with this female type, the male should not be round or concaved in the back, but should be nearly straight in the back. A slight concave at the base of tail is sufficient to give the back the necessary length and flatness and at the same time save it from being too angular in appearance. For females of this correct type see pictures of 1st pullet at New York, December, 1911, and 1st pullet at Crystal Palace, Lon-

don, December, 1913, on pages 79 and 82. For correct back line in both male and female see pair of Silver Campines in the colored frontispiece. The back of the Campine should not be too broad and coarse at shoulders. It is important that the plumage should be long, especially in the male, the longer the saddle feathers, the better. I again repeat, this length of plumage, especially in the male is important. The barring should be closely examined on the back. The black bar should make about four white bars in the females and from three to four white bars in the males. In the males the barring of the back is naturally V-shaped, but in other sections as well as in all sections of the female, the barring should be "slightly V-shaped." The black bar should be free from a gray or brown intermediate bar, and should be of a greenish lustrous hue. This soundness and lustre of the back barring is found in high-grade cockerels and cocks of both varieties and constitutes the perfect color.

Tail: The male's tail should be carried rather low. To attain this style it is necessary to breed plenty of furnishing, that is coverts and lesser sickles. It should be understood that the Campine male is "heney." Such a color-type as we see in the Silver and Golden Campines is used by the breeders of Silver and Golden Penciled Hamburgs to breed pullets. The effeminate characters of short back plumage and tails without sickles are not wanted in the Campines. We want to retain a color of plumage identical to that of the female, but breed as much of the cock feathering as possible. A male's tail that is nearly as devoid of furnishing as a hen's is positively undesirable. Moreover, it will stand up high and the stiff main tail feathers will stand up like a brush. With a furnishing of covering feathers, a lower, more graceful sweep and carriage of tail is secured, as if there was weight added to hold down the main tail feathers. In securing length and furnish of tail it is desirable that quality be secured as well as quantity. Long sickles are often seen that are not barred but are sort of a mealy gray and brown. This is the Braekel tail, and while it contains quantity in sufficiency, the quality is such that a shorter pair of sickles well barred should always win in preference. The tail of the Silver Campine female in the colored frontispiece is well carried. It is expanded just right and is carried out and rather low as is typical of the best pullets.

WINNER 2ND PRIZE CKL. MADISON SQUARE GARDEN DEC. 1913. OWNED AND BRED BY MARTLING HENNERY, RIDGEFIELD, N.J.

One of the smartest and most promising males in the cockerel class in Campine row at the 1913 Madison Square Garden Show was the winner of second. He was a combination of vigor and style, with good black and white barring and the whitest neck hackle in the class—a point that has proved very rare on specimens being so close to the Standard amount of color. It appears that this is going to be one of the hardest points to produce on birds with Standard body markings.—F. L. Sewell.

Wings: The Campine's wings when opened are large. They should not effect a brawny appearance at the shoulder, however. The bird should not be thick and coarse through the shoulders. The best barring of the long wing feathers is found in the secondaries. The primaries, especially of the males, are inclined to be white; in the female the primaries are inclined to be black or peppery-black on the wide side of the quill, while the narrow side of web is white. Such wings are defective. The primary coverts in the males occasionally grow very long and are sometimes wonderfully barred. There are two serious defects seen in the wings of males. First is the color defect of secondaries not being barred. This effects a white wing bay and since the Campine is a barred bird, save neck, this white flat-iron against the side of the bird breaks the harmony of the color. Such a bird will also have whitish flights and should be classed as very weak in wing. The other serious defect is one of type, seen by aid of the wings and measured by them. The Campine male should be long in body and when so short that the curved in points of the two wings meet behind the body, the bird is poorly formed and is not deserving of a place in the prize list of a big show or the breeding yard of the critical fancier.

Breast: The breast of both sexes should be full and round. The formation as commonly found is good. The usual defects of the breast are in the color. The breast should be barred. The feathers should not end in a crescentic spangle or ring of black, while the rest of the web is white. The barring in this section should be straight across the feather and sound. When this is secured, the fact that the white bar (or golden bar) is nearly as wide as the black bar, should cause no dissatisfaction with the breeder or penalty at the hands of the judge. Rather, let them look to see that the barring runs into the throat and that the throat is not washy. Also, that the barring is sound down where the harder surfaced breast feathers join the softer surfaced fluff feathers. Here the black bar should be firm or positive, not running gray; and the white bar should also be pure.

Body and Fluff: The soft plumage on the sides of the body should be barred. The fluff at the rear is gray. When viewed from the rear, the body should not be sharp. The underline of the male body from throat around underneath to tail should be crescentic. This roundness saves the Campine male from being oblong or angular and is important.

Under Color: In all sections slate.

Legs and Toes: In color these sections should be blue. The bone should be fine, for the Campine is a wanderer, a picker and not a scratcher. The shanks should be round and the scales fine and neatly laid on. The condition of the shanks is important; a leg with any tendency to scabbiness should be deemed so seriously defective that the Campine would not be entitled to a prize. The thighs and shanks should be rather long and the bone of the thighs, as well as that of the shanks, rather light, giving a slender appearance and agility of action. Birds that are full in body and short in legs are too heavy, too squatty to be typical. They again partake of the Braekel.

Size: Over sized birds are not desirable. The weights as adopted by the club are as follows:

Cock ....6 lbs.   Cockerel ....5 lbs.
Hen ....4 lbs.   Pullet ....3½ lbs.

These weights are a safe guide for judges and breeders. Birds of this size will reproduce themselves, grow fast and lay well.

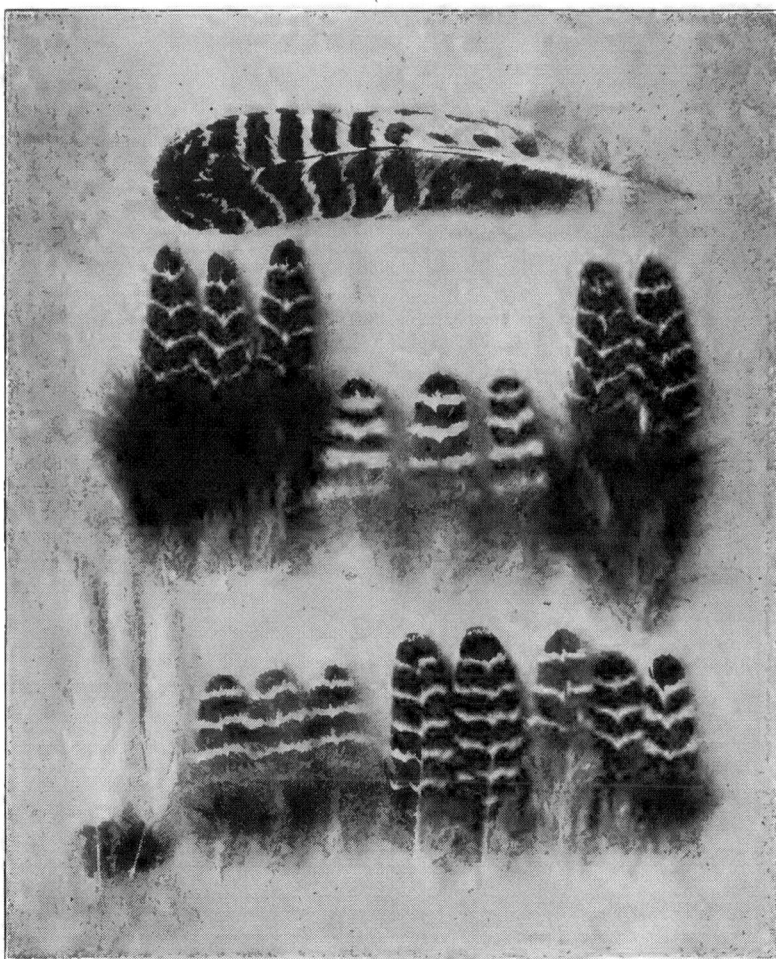

FEATHERS FROM WINNING CAMPINES

This plate of Campine plumage shows specimen feathers from winning birds belonging to M. R. Jacobus, Box 3, Ridgefield, N. J., which were plucked from them by Mr. Herman Sonders, poultryman for Mr. Jacobus. These sample feathers clearly illustrate the broad black bar and narrow white penciling now being selected in show quality specimens. The three feathers in the center which show black and white bars of equal width, are from the breast of a Silver Campine. These are very good breast feathers. Frequently the breast, especially the upper part, fails in barring. This deficiency in breast color is usually accompanied by a white hackle. To maintain the silvery white neck plumage and strengthen the black barring of the breast is proving an interesting task. Ideal hackle feathers from the Silver Campine male are shown at the bottom and at the left of the feather plate. They illustrate the slate colored base and desirable white surface. These feathers were selected during the show season of 1911-12.

The Ideal Campine of Today

Writing theFirst Campine Standard—Obeying the Wishes and Opinions of Campine Breeders—An Explanation of the Campine Club Standard and the Steps That Lead Lead to It.

By F. L. Platt

W E WILL take up those questions of body-type and color-type that are of interest and importance to Campine breeders of today. Some will read this article with a view to getting the opinions of the writer; some have studied his awards at the New York Show with a view to getting his opinions. But, let us go back farther than this, let us look at those conditions from which opinions took their form; they are hardly perceivable now to the unguided eye, but by them alone the course of the Campine Standard was governed.

The first Campine Standard was written in our room in the old Union Square Hotel in New York. M. R.

1st prize Silver Campine pullet, Crystal Palace Show, London, 1913. Rev. Jones judged the class. Here is the modern type Campine female, showing correct stations, length of body, and spread and carriage of tail. As the judge at the Madison Square Garden Show, New York, 1911, 1912 and 1913, this has been the type that we have persistently favored.

Jacobus had made an appointment to meet us and there on a cold marble topped table a standard was written. He put it in his pocket to have it typewritten next day, then printed. He and other breeders were selling eggs for hatching, also stock. Customers wanted to cull, wanted to exhibit, judges wanted to judge, so of necessity a Standard was born, a law by which to judge and breed.

"What an opportunity to impress your own opinions on the destiny of a breed." Ah, you lose the philosophy of law making. It is one thing to write a law but, that

is not all. The National Assembly at the time of the French revolution learned and illustrated this lesson. They could build a constitution, "Constitutions enough, but the frightful difficulty is of getting men to come and live in them * * * The constitution, the laws, or the prescribed Habits of Acting, that men will live under, is one which images their convictions—their faith as to this wondrous universe and what rights, duties, capabilities they have there * * * Other laws * * * are usurpations which men do not obey, but rebel against and abolish by their earliest convenience." Thus writes Carlyle in his history of the revolution. There is waste of energy in struggling against the tendencies of the times. The successful law maker is the keen interpreter of the times; he "images the convictions" of the people as Carlyle says—he reflects the temper of the age. So it is that the general opinion, the general spirit, the ideals of those breeders who are in the ascendant—these are to be garnered and systematized—these are the rudiments of a Standard.

The judges, they will do their turn with a certain individualism, but do not look too much at their peculiarities of preference and too little at the spirit of the times. Do they regulate the course of fashion? They are but the interpreters. All about them opinions are forming, preferences are becoming established by which alone the course is ultimately governed. The judge must have a just appreciation of the spirit of the times or he will exhaust his resources struggling against it.

That is true of the standard maker. Here nothing could be more shallow than obstinacy, of pretending to be guided by principals when in reality the mind is subjugated by prejudice. The standard maker should shape his work, not according to a hasty deduction from a general knowledge of breeds, but according to the wishes and experience of the breeders of the breed, whom he represents and whom he is bound to obey.

This thought, Edmund Burke expressed in his letter to the sheriffs of Bristol, saying: "In effect, to follow, not to force, the public inclination; to give a direction, a form, a technical dress and a specific sanction to the general sense of the community—is the true end of legislature." Did the writers of the Campine Standard follow "the public inclination," did they sanction "the general sense" of the breeders; does the standard give to the shifting agency which we call the "Improved Campine," that form and phrase of perfection which is in the eye of the breeders? If so, the standard was well made, it will last; breeders will breed to it and it will outlive the petty talk of an "Eastern" and "Western" type of Campines. For the fundamentals of the Campine Standard are then true, the original analysis did indeed disclose the rudiments and the foundation is sound on which breeders may build the superstructure. Let us see.

If we would understand how opinions are formed, we should understand the nature of our subject and observe the force of circumstances. Thus our inquiry into what is the correct type of body and character of barring, becomes enlarged into a study of the history of the Campine Standard by which each Standard requirement is explained by making plain the course that led to it, by making plain that these requirements are not single and isolated, the result of blind chance or dominating impulse, but that each is connected with a preceding fact and all are linked together. Thus will we cover those questions that are of interest and importance to Campine breeders today and show why the Standard is as it is and is, we believe, as it should be.

The Campine Standard Explained

Let us begin with the name of the breed. It is that of the district in Belgium from which the breed first came. In the southern part of Belgium there is another breed, larger, and in many respects similar. But, the Campine was first to be imported into England because it came more under the range of observation. It is a small fowl that had for a hundred years been kept in the peasants' dooryards and now like a centennial cactus flower shines forth. But, not for long; at the dawn of the new century the flower is closing, its pollen blown as waste. Then from the Braekel district comes promise of perpetual splendor. The English take the hen-feathered Braekel, a few agreeing, many dissenting and propagate the off-shoot of the old flower. And so the Campine, now half Braekel, in nature hen-feathered, is given a new flower pot that it may have more room for its roots and more sunshine for its head.

But, the Belgian type; those long flowing sickles, well furnished tails. The new hen-feathered birds, too many of them have a tail that stands up like a brush. Lower tails with weight to hold them down, more furnishings, longer sickles, more and longer coverts, were quickly in need.

The new Campine male is a barred Campine. Still the Braekel tail frequently appears on specimens, a long tail but devoid of barring. It is not an accomplishment in breeding, it is furnish of plumage at the expense of character of markings. It is not a good tail. The Standard tail is well furnished and barred.

A barred bird—what then is more important than the barring or perhaps, to be more exact, penciling. It is most conspicuously seen on the back so this section is given a color valuation of six points. It is important, too, that the plumage over the hips should be as long as possible, since it carries this wonderful color and it is important that the male have as much furnish here as possible.

The Belgian type has a white wing bay; but the barred type—shall its secondaries not also be barred so that when closed the color scheme will be carried out around the entire body? That will mean to carry the barring into the flights and this has been done.

How striking is a white neck in contrast to the green lustre of the body. The white hackle, however, is accompanied by a weakness in throat and breast marking. On the farms of Campine plenty of white necks are to be seen, but no well marked breasts and throats. Barring up to the gills therefore shows considerate breeding and a bird with a white neck and washy throat is only a rooster. Let the color run into the hackle a bit. We must not be too abrupt in the demand that the barring stop at the cape and begin with the hackle. We must bear a bit with nature. This section, therefore, although important in setting off the bird, in giving contrast to its color pattern, shall be valued at five points and the cuts made with leniency.

On the next page is shown a Silver Penciled Hamburg pullet and pullet-breeding cockerel bred by Harry Turton, England. It has been said that Campinists are breeding the duplicate of this feather pattern except on coarser lines. The time element is vastly stronger in the Hamburg and we may look to it for that perfection which is not quick to associate itself with shorter pedigrees. In the male the pure whiteness of hackle, the sound throat barring and the narrow, distinct white penciling that divides with precision the black ground color, denote long years of thoughtful breeding. The green lustre to the black is not vividly conveyed by the picture, but the English breed it, even in their Campines so bright and deep that it is not unlike a gloss enameling the feather.

The picture of the Hamburg pullet shows an elegance of plumage that plainly indicates many years of selective breeding. The beautifully regular and even spacing of black and white is carried through the back and to the very tips of the tail feathers. In "Our Poul-

3rd Silver Campine pullet at the Crystal Palace, London, 1910. Bred by Rev. Jones, and in her day was said to possess an ideal type.

try" Harrison Weir tells of the penciled pullets of seventy years ago. "Sometimes," he says, "only the two upper feathers of the tail had these elegant traceries." The approach to perfection has been made by the most skillful, patient breeding. Yet, the coloring invades the lower neck feathers. Let Campinists note this.

Standing in competition with such a finished breed as this, how shall the new Campine fare? Did it not borrow some of the size of the Braekel, and since it is a larger fowl cannot its larger individual feathers carry a wider, heavier bar? This will distinguish it. And so it does. We find a heavier body in the Campine. To refer again to the picture of the Hamburg male, let Campinists insist on a heavier body that the wing flights may not extend like swords beyond the fluff. In judging Campine males I would always see, if necessary, would turn the bird around to see that the wing flights were not longer than the body. Unlike the Hamburg, the Campine is not wholly a fowl of feather properties. Thus we arrive at last to the standard description of the body, which contains in few words what time and

Silver Penciled Hamburg pullet and pullet-breeding cockerel bred by Harry Turton, England.

destiny have decreed. It reads: "Body moderate length and fairly deep. Not a sharp appearing body from behind."

The Campine must be distinct; is there an indication of the Hamburg; let us know it, and we will cull against it. So we find the red eye of the Hamburg a serious defect in the Campine. This seriousness, however, applies with especial emphasis to the Silver. I do not think that I have placed a red eyed Silver at New York in three years, but I have yet to find the iris of a Golden cockerel's eye that did not fade to red as he became a cock. This is a good point for American breeders to know, for it must be admitted that as a whole, we do not acquaint ourselves with the nature of breeds and as a consequence have the most bookish and mechanical Standards in the world.

If we could have it, our birds would be turned out on a lathe. This spirit was quite noticeable when the new type of Campine was first shown here. The type had its beginning in 1904. To perfect the body and feather properties, the English had neglected the comb. Had given it a valuation of three points. Without giving credit to these other properties, the combs were loudly criticised when the birds were first shown at New York —as if pickled cocks' combs was the end and purpose for which chickens were kept.

This tendency of the people was not to be balked, however, and combs have been finely improved. And the Standard carries the influence of the English mind, for unlike the Leghorn's comb, which we value at ten points, the Campine's comb is valued at eight points in the new 1915 edition of the American Standard of Perfection. So it is that a policy that once has become established, even though it is later modified, continues to exert an influence over a long period.

How much more firmly established must be the characters of a breed which are due to centuries of environment. In the modern Campine we have a composite or two sets of characters. Shall one be dominant and the other recessive, or shall they be blended and a new Campine come forth? There are the concave lines of the Campine; petite, graceful; there are the ob-

long lines of the Braekel, but many of this race are too full of fluff and short of shank. For a time the Campine lines were held, as is shown by the illustration of the 3rd Crystal Palace pullet, 1910, which was the property of Rev. E. Lewis Jones, and said by him to show the proper type. We find him in 1913, however, placing first prize at the Dairy on a pullet belonging to Miss Edwards, of a new type. It is the type that the American Club Standard calls for; the type that has been set as ideal at the American Campine Club shows. If ever there was an improved type of Campine, this is it. We hear it said by outsiders that this type takes too much of the Minorca—as if the Minorca were a mean race. Let us say it embodies the alertness of the Campine, the length and somewhat of the size of the Braekel without its coarse shoulders, stubby legs and full fluff. It is distinct from the Hamburg.

The lines of the Leghorn have influenced some of the recruits to the Campine fancy in America. But, the improved Campine is not a Leghorn. Its back should be as the American Standard says: "Back rather long, declining slightly to tail, not too broad at shoulders and narrowing very slightly to tail." A sharply concaved back is a feature of some of the winning males, you say. Quite true, but such birds win because their color merits over-balance their shape defects, it being impossible in a new breed to find the specimens strictly uniform. So it happens that the best "all round" bird is often the winner. It is the tendency, however, the tendency towards an ideal and what that ideal is, that ultimately matters.

The American Campine Club Standard drawn up on the basis that if the male is to have a concave back, there must be mates that can breed such males—reads in the male description as in the female back description given above. The two sexes are therefore uniform and the type consistent. It is a useful type, putting strength into the little Campine type, putting the spirit of alertness into the Braekel. And so, from the material in hand, it has been made, the hand of the moulders being guided by common belief that "type is intimately connected with the economic qualities of the bird."

Judging Campines

The Author of this Article has Judged the Campine Classes at Leading Shows of the East, Including Philadelphia, Boston, New York State Fair—Difficulties in Judging a New Breed—Three Bars on the Surface is Enough—Some Penciling at the Base of the Hackle Should be Allowed—The Way the Tail Joins the Back Should be Carefully Observed—Low Stationed Birds Not Wanted—Every Bird is Entitled to Proper Consideration at the Hands of the Judge—Be Decisive.

By M. L. Chapman, Brown's Mills, N. J.

THIS article was written just previous to the admission of the Campine to the American Standard of Perfection and was revised just after recognition was accorded them by the American Poultry Association at Chicago, August 11th to 14th, 1914. While the American Campine Club has had a standard for the guidance of judges and breeders, there have been several points of agitation that could only be settled by the A. P. A. Standard makers. In the past we have had to deal with Campine matters largely from the standpoint of the intent of the leading breeders as to what, in their opinion, should constitute a perfect Campine.

It seemed to be the wish of many Campine breeders that their favorites should be classed with the Mediterranean breeds. If this had been done Campines would have to have been judged by the same scale of points as other Mediterranean breeds. However, a new class has been provided for the Campines, namely, a Continental class, and a scale of points has been adopted similar to that used in the Club Standard. The greatest difference in value of sections in the Mediterranean scale of points from that adopted by the Campine Club has been in head points, the former allotting 35 points to the head sections, while the latter alloted 26 of the 100 points. I mention these matters so that not only what follows may be better understood, but that the difficulties that have attended the satisfactory judging of Campine classes in the past may be appreciated.

To begin with the head points; the comb should be medium in size, single, straight and upright, slightly following the shape of the neck but not laying on the neck, serrated into five points, the points should be shaped like a sharpened lead pencil rather than wedge shaped. To be considered perfect a Campine's comb need not be quite as fine in texture as the comb of a White Leghorn. Many Campines have a six point comb and if the comb has a blade of good length six points become the bird as well as would five points. The standard used to allow either five or six points as perfect for the Mediterranean

breeds and from the standpoint of true beauty, one is as good as another. The change to five points was made because it was thought that both could not be consistently classed as perfect. The point is that a six point comb if good otherwise should not be penalized very heavily.

There is one thing certain; the Campine breeders have got to improve the combs on their male birds. Considerable leniency has been allowed the breeders in this respect by the judges during the past few years, but the time has arrived when the law in reference to combs standing upright should be enforced.

The eye should be large and prominent. The dark eye is one of the breed characteristics and it is quite important that it should be as dark as possible. The eye color will fade some with age and this fault should not be penalized as heavily in an old bird as would the same eye in a cockerel or pullet. Wattles should be medium in length, well rounded and free from wrinkles. Ear lobes should be smooth, medium in size, broadened almond in shape, white in color and nicely enameled. The neck should be of medium length, nicely arched, and abundant hackle. The color of the head and neck, in my opinion, is best described by silvery white. Many of the best specimens answer this description and such a color with its burnished metallic appearance harmonizes with the general color scheme of the breed. The undercolor of the hackle should be slate. A pure white hackle on a bird with good back pattern and a well barred breast is very rare, indeed. The writer never remembers seeing one and I have handled the winners at the large eastern shows for a number of years. Right here is where the judge has to exercise discretion and should remember that both back and breast are given more points in color value than the hackle. To make a long story short, slight ticking or tipping of the hackle at the base or part that flows over the shoulders really detracts but little from the beauty of the bird and should be penalized very lightly.

Some judges and breeders are under the impression

This is one of two cockerels shown at Boston that were pronounced by Campine men to be the best exhibited in 1913-14. He has good type, carriage and head, and is remarkably regular in his markings. The sheen of the black—all that is to be desired.—Louis Paul Graham.

that a pure white hackle should be given preference over everything else. There is nothing in the Standard adopted by the club March 7, 1913, nor will there be anything in the 1915 A. P. A. Standard, to warrant this and it is the opinion of the leading breeders now that it is better to have slight ticking in the hackle and a bird well barred in all sections than a pure white hackle and weak barring in breast.

The color of the back is really the keynote to the whole color scheme of each bird. Many of the best breeders and judges have maintained that the color of back should be given a greater value than the color of any other section and the trend of opinion is in that direction. Without a good back your chance of winning in the show room is poor, indeed. The dark bar should have a lustrous green sheen and should be four times the width of the white bar. The white bar should have clear cut edges. Up to the present time a more or less V-shaped white bar has been accepted on a par with a straight bar. It seemed practically certain that when the breed was admitted to the A. P. A. Standard breeders would have to say which type of barring they preferred, as both styles could not be accepted as perfect. The matter of obtaining the sense of the breeders on this important feature was left to the American Campine Club, with the result that a description was decided upon for use in the 1915 Standard, as follows: The bar shall be "slightly V-shaped."

The judges should examine all specimens carefully for what is called mossiness or blurred barring of a brownish color, in the back. First class specimens present a sharp clean cut barred effect to the eye that is very beautiful.

I have before me feathers from the back of several noted winners. Most of them have three bars on each feather. It is enough. I hope the Campine breeders will never go in for barring to the skin. The undercolor of the back should be dark slate. Practically all wild birds that have a brilliant top color have a slate undercolor, and it seems to be best suited to reflect a brilliant top color such as the Campines have in the lustrous dark bar. The barring in the wings and tail should be wider than those in the other sections. The majority of the males do not show, as yet, very good tail and wing barring. The best specimens have well barred tail coverts and sickles. The females, especially in their pullet year, show well barred wings and tails, the curve of the back and the way the back and tail join together should be carefully noted by the judge. A good back and tail add as much or more to the appearance of a bird as any other sec-

SECOND PRIZE SILVER CAMPINE COCKEREL
BOSTON—JAN. 1914
Owned by C. A. PHIPPS · · · · Wayland, Mass.

This cockerel is an exceptionally well marked bird; brilliant sheeny black and white, regular markings, good head and good type, although a little too high in tail to meet the standard of Campine tail carriage. Taken altogether, he is a worthy second to the extraordinarily fine first prize Silver cockerel.—Louis Paul Graham.

tion. High tails have been one of the faults of the breed. A bird with a very high tail has no beauty and the defect should be penalized heavily. In order to get the well spread tail that is so admired on the male birds, they should have seven feathers on each side, besides the sickle feathers. Some females that spread their tails well, look all right with seven feathers on a side. Females from which you expect to breed show males should have eight feathers on a side. A large powerful wing is one of the characteristics of the breed.

A breast perfect in shape is hard to get in any breed. Fortunately most Campines have well shaped breasts. It should be deep, well rounded, carried well forward and the keel bone nearly horizontal. One defect that is sometimes found is that the keel bone runs up in the air too sharply, which makes too much daylight under the breast and gives the bird the appearance of being poorly balanced. The dark and white bars on the breast should be of equal width. Broken barring—bars running only half way across feathers—and in some cases penciled instead of barred, are the defects that the judge should look for; these are serious defects and should be penalized accordingly. A Campine should show some thigh underneath his body when viewed from the side, not enough to present a leggy appearance, but enough to stop short of what would be described as a low stationed bird. Do not make the mistake of thinking that any dark color for shanks and feet will do. The color described by the Standard is leaden blue. This color, when seen at its best, adds materially to the beauty of the bird, and if shanks are not leaden blue they should be cut accordingly.

I have not attempted to say how much the cut should be for the various defects, but simply to give the faults most likely to be found and to indicate as to their relative seriousness. Just a suggestion that applies to the judging of all breeds. Every bird is entitled to proper consideration and should be allowed opportunity to pose themselves naturally. It may take several trips carefully up and down the aisles to give all the birds a proper chance. I generally do this first and make all my checks, as to shape, etc., before I start handling any of the birds, for the reason that you will occasionally find a wild bird, or one with a bad disposition, that will cry out and make disturbance enough to frighten all birds in that vicinity and after such a disturbance none of the birds will do themselves justice for some time. Another thing, do not get your impression of a bird's shape while you have one hand in the coop bearing down hard on his tail. If a bird is quiet and you work long enough on him you can pat and push him into the shape you want and he will probably hold the pose for you for the time being, but you are not supposed to do that. Walk along the aisle and quietly attract the attention of each bird and let him show you what he has got, but do not give any osteopathic treatments. After you have satisfied your mind as to shape, start at one end of the line and go carefully over each bird for disqualification, etc. If you have several birds off about equal merit, compare them side by side and section by section as to color, then empty enough coops to line them up together and compare them for shape, consider everything carefully and make your decision promptly and on the spot.

The writer has had the honor of judging the Campine classes at some of the large shows in the past and during a time when there was little in the written law to go by and some difference of opinion as to what constituted a good Campine. I do not feel that I can close without a word of appreciation for the sportsman qualities that have always been displayed by the Campine breeders in their acceptance of my awards.

Rose Comb Silver Campines

By F. L. Platt

ROSE Comb Campines, both Silver and Golden, have been known in Belgium for many years. Dr. H. P. Clarke, of Indianapolis, was the first to draw the attention of Americans to these Rose Combs, he being attracted to some Rose Comb Silver Campines while exhibiting Games in France and Belgium. These birds were hen-feathered and it was because of this feature, which he believed to be of great breeding value in the production of females, that he fancied them. This was before the advent of the modern English-type Silver Campine, and Dr. Clarke in his early appreciation of this type, is truly to be considered one of the pioneers in Campine history.

In 1911 and 1912 when the English type Campines were becoming popular in America and the exportation of stock from England was at its height, the envy of the Belgians was aroused. While the Campine was a native of Belgium, practically no stock was being imported from Belgium by Americans, but the English alone were reaping the benefit of the "boom."

The Belgians were aroused. They charged the English with infusing Hamburg blood in their stock. There can be no doubt but what the charge was justified by facts, notwithstanding the argument of the English.

The controversy was led by Madame A. F. Van Schelle on the Belgian side, and replied to by Rev. E. Lewis Jones for the English. It waxed warm and was carried the rounds of the English poultry press and into the leading Belgian weekly, Chasse et Peche, of Brussels.

The Rose Comb Campine was the center of the controversy. Did the Rose Comb come from the Hamburg cross? Yes, said the Belgians; no, said the English.

The issue, however, is no longer a live one. It has been shown that Rose Comb Campines have been bred off and on in Belgium for years, and that Rose Comb Campines have been hatched from eggs of English Silver Campines.

We reprint the following two letters on the subject of Rose Comb Silver Campines:

68 Studley Road, Clapham, London, Eng.
Editor R. P. J.:—
I was much interested in the article by Mr. Platt on Campines in your April issue.

Mr. Platt says that he did not see a Rose Comb Campine in Belgium, but perhaps he will recollect calling upon me with the Rev. Lewis Jones when he was in England and seeing some Rose Combs that I had bred. I think he rather liked them. I still have some, although I killed a good many.

This is how I came to get them. I had been breeding Campines for some years when in 1910 one, a hen, came with a rose comb. I mated her with a single comb cockerel and most of her progeny came with rose combs. I still have the original rose comb hen, which by the way, I christened Bleriot on account of her flying propensities.   Yours faithfully,
S. E. DUNKIN,
(Vice-President Campine Club.)

Monsey, N. Y., Sept. 23, 1913.
Editor Campine Herald:—
Dear Sir:—It may interest your readers to learn that I have (much to my surprise) two Rose Comb Silver Campine sports, male and female, hatched early in July; being a late brood they were allowed to roam at large with the hen, consequently they did not come under my notice until a few days ago. Like all my stock they were bred from imported English prize winners and as I breed nothing but Silver Campines an interesting field of speculation is opened up as to why these two particular birds should have rose combs, when their brothers and sisters (a few hundred in number) have bred true to type; perhaps some of our Mendelism friends will come forward with an explanation.
Truly yours,
E. J. GIDMAN.

Made in the USA
Las Vegas, NV
22 February 2022